孫子兵法

I

Sun Tzu's
Art of War
Playbook
Volume 1 of 9:
Positions

Gary Gagliardi

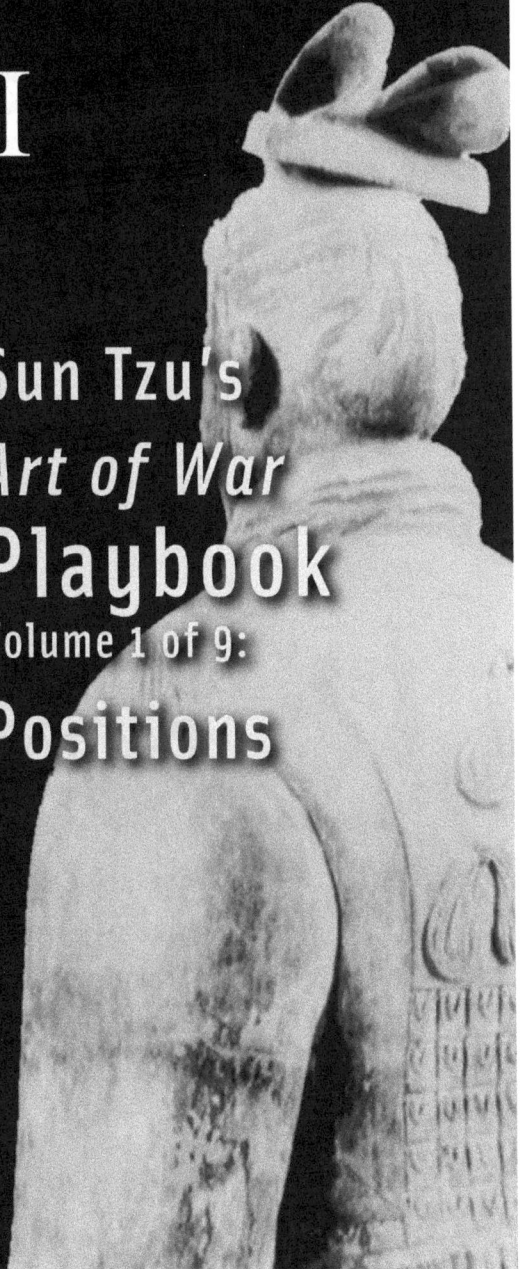

Sun Tzu's Art of War Playbook

Volume One:
Positions

by Gary Gagliardi
The Science of Strategy Institute
Clearbridge Publishing

Published by
Science of Strategy Institute, Clearbridge Publishing
    suntzus.com   scienceofstrategy.org

Library of Congress Control Number: 2014909969
First Print Edition
Also sold as Sun Tzu's Warrior Rule Book
Copyright 2010, 2011, 2012, 2013, 2014 Gary Gagliardi
ISBN 978-1-929194-76-6(13-digit) 1-929194-76-5 (10-digit)

Originally published as a series of articles on the Science of Strategy Website, scienceofstratregy.org. and
later as an ebook on various sites. Ebook ISBN 978-1-929194-63-6

PO Box 33772, Seattle, WA 98133
Phone: (206)542-8947 Fax: (206)546-9756
beckyw@clearbridge.com
garyg@scienceofstrategy.org

Manufactured in the United States of America.
Interior and cover graphic design by Dana and Jeff Wincapaw.
Original Chinese calligraphy by Tsai Yung, Green Dragon Arts, www.greendragonarts.com.

Publisher's Cataloging-in-Publication Data
Sun-tzu, 6th cent. B.C.
Strategy, positioning
    [Sun-tzu ping fa, English]
    Volume One: Art of War Playbook / Sun Tzu and Gary Gagliardi.
    p.197 cm. 23
    Includes introduction to basic competitive philosophy of Sun Tzu

Clearbridge Publishing's books may be purchased for business, for any promotional use,
or for special sales.

Contents

Playbook Overview

Note: This overview is provided for those who have not read the previous volume of Sun Tzu's Art of War Playbook. *It provides an brief overview of the work in general and the general concepts framing the first volume.*

Sun Tzu's **The Art of War** is less a "book" in the modern Western sense than it is an outline for a course of study. Like Euclid's Geometry, simply reading the work teaches us very little. Sun Tzu wrote in in a tradition that expected each line and stanza to be studied in the context of previous statements to build up the foundation for understanding later statements.

To make this work easier for today's readers to understand, we developed the **Strategy Playbook**, the Science of Strategy Institute (SOSI) guidebook to explaining Sun Tzu's strategy in the more familiar format of a series of explanations with examples. These lessons are framed in the context of modern competition rather than ancient military warfare.

This Playbook is the culmination of over a decade of work breaking down Sun Tzu's principles into a series of step-by-step practical articles by the Institute's multiple award-winning author and founder, Gary Gagliardi. The original *Art of War* was written for military generals who understood the philosophical concepts of ancient China, which in itself is a practical hurdle that most modern readers cannot clear. Our Art of War Playbook is written for today's reader. It puts Sun Tzu's ideas into everyday, practical language.

The Playbook defines a new science of strategic competition aimed at today's challenges. This science of competition is designed as the complementary opposite of the management science that is taught in most business schools. This science starts, as Sun Tzu did himself, by defining a better, more complete vocabulary for discussing competitive situations. It connects the timeless ideas of Sun Tzu to today's latest thinking in business, mathematics, and psychology.

The entire Playbook consists of two hundred and thirty articles describing over two-thousand interconnected key methods. These articles are organized into nine different areas of strategic skill from understanding positioning to defending vulnerabilities. All together this makes up over a thousand pages of material.

Playbook Access

The Playbook's most up-to-date version is available as separate articles on our website. Live links make it easy to access the connections between various articles and concepts. If you become a SOSI Member, you can access any Playbook article at any time and access their links.

However, at the request of our customers, we also offer these articles as a series of nine eBooks. Each of the nine sections of the entire Playbook makes up a separate eBook, Playbook Parts One Through Nine. These parts flow logically through the Progress Cycle of listen-aim-move-claim (see illustration). Because of the dynamic nature of the on-line version, these eBooks are not going to be as current as the on-line version. You can see a outline of current Playbook articles here and, generally, the eBook version will contain most of the same material in the same order.

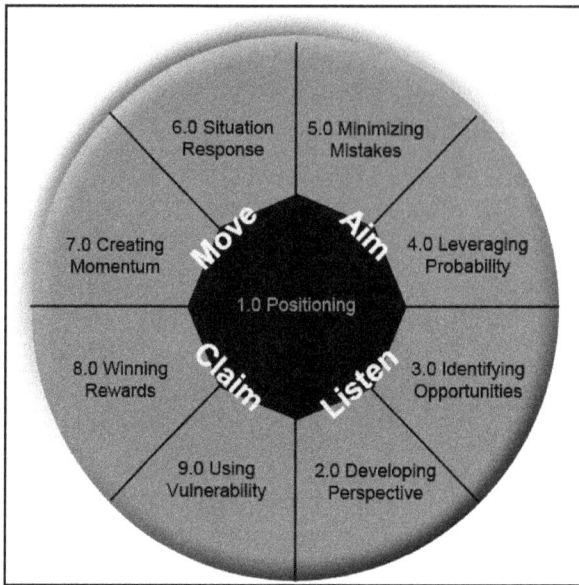

Nine categories of strategic skills define cycle that advances our positions:

1. Comparing Positions,

2. Developing Perspective,

3. Identifying Opportunities,

4. Leveraging Probability,

5. Minimizing Mistakes,

6. Responding To Situations,

7. Creating Momentum,

8. Winning Rewards, And

9. Defending Vulnerabilities.

Playbook Structure and Design

These articles are written in standard format including 1) the general principle, 2) the situation, 3) the opportunity, 4) the list of specific Art of War key methods breaking down the general principle into a series of actions, and 5) an illustration of the application of each of those key methods to a specific competitive situation. Key methods are written generically to apply to every competitive arena (business, personal life, career, sports, relationships, etc.) with each specific illustrations drawn from one of these areas.

A number identifies where each article appears in Playbook Structure. For example, the article 2.1.3 Strategic Deception is the third article in the first section of the second book in the nine volumes of the Strategy Playbook. In our on-line version, these links are live, clicking on them brings you to the article itself. We provide them because the interconnection of concepts is important in learning Sun Tzu's system.

Playbook Training

Training in Sun Tzu's warrior skills does not entail memorizing all these principles. Instead, these concepts are used to develop exercises and tools that allow trainees to put this ideas in practice. While each rule is useful, the heart of Sun Tzu system is the methods that connect all the principles together. Training in these principles is designed to develop a gut instinct for how Sun Tzu's strategy is used in different situations to produce success. Principles are interlinked because they describe a comprehensive conceptual mental model. Warrior Class training puts trainees in a situation where they must constantly make decisions, rewarding them for making decisions consist with winning productively instead of destructively.

About Positions

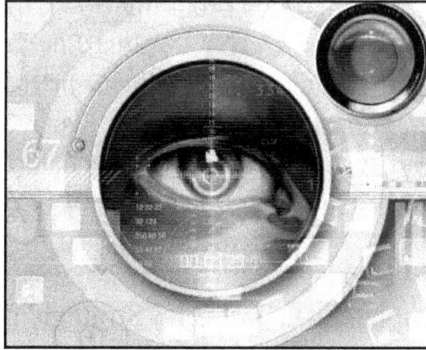

This first volume of Sun Tzu's Playbook focuses on teaching us the nature of strategic positions. "Position awareness" gives you a framework for understanding your strategic situation relative to the conditions around you. It enables you to see your position as part of a larger environment constructed of other positions and the raw elements that create positions. Master Sun Tzu's system of comparing positions, you can understand which aspect of your position are secure and which are the most dynamic and likely to change.

Traditional strategy defines a "position" as a comparison of situations. Game theory defines is as the current decision point that is arrive at as the sum or result of all previous decisions, both yours and those of others. Sun Tzu's methods of positioning awareness are different. They force you to see yourself in the eyes of others. Using these techniques, you broaden your perspective by gathering a range of viewpoints. In a limited sense, the scope of your position defines your area of control within your larger environment. In traditional strategy, five elements--mission, climate, ground, command, and methods--define the dimensions in which competitors can be compared.

Competition as Comparison

Sun Tzu saw that success is based on comparisons. This comparison must take place whenever a choice is made. For Sun Tzu, competition means a comparison of alternative choices or "positions". Battles are won by positioning before they are fought. These positions provide choices for everyone involved. Good positions discourage others from attacking you and invite them to support you. Sun Tzu's system teaches us how to systematically build up our positions to win success in the easiest way possible.

Competing positions are compared on the basis many elements, both objective and subjective. Sun Tzu's strategy is to identify these points of comparison and to understand how to leverage them. Learning Sun Tzu's strategy requires learning the details of how positions are compared and advanced. Sun Tzu taught that fighting to "sort things out" is a foolish way to find learn the strengths and weaknesses of a position. Conflict to tear down opposing positions is the most costly way to win competitive comparisons.

Today's More Competitive World

In the complex, chaotic world of today, we can easily get trapped into destructive rather than productive situations. Even our smallest decisions can have huge impact on our future. The problem is that we are trained for yesterday's world of workers, not today's world of warriors. We are trained in the linear thinking of planning in predictable, hierarchical world. This thinking applies less and less to today's networked, more competitive world.

Following a plan is the worker's skill of working in pre-defined functions in an internal, stable, controlled environment. The competitive strategy of Sun Tzu is the warrior's skill of making good decisions about conditions in complex, fast-changing, competitive environments. Sun Tzu's strategic system teaches us to adapt to the unexpected events that are becoming more and more common in our lives. We live in a world where fewer and fewer key events are planned. Navigating our new world of external challenges requires a different set of skills.

Most of us make our decisions without any understanding of competition. The result is that most of us lose as many battles as we win, never making consistent progress. Events buffet us, turning us in one direction and then the other. Too often, we end up repeating our past patterns of mistakes.

The Science of Strategy Institute teaches you the warrior's skills of adaptive response. There are many organizations that teach planning and organization. The Institute is one of the few places in the world you can get learn competitive thinking, and the only place in the world, with a comprehensive Playbook.

Seeing Situations Differently

Sun Tzu taught that a warrior's decision-making was a matter of reflex. As we develop our strategic decision-making skills, the critical conditions in situations simply "pop" out at us. This isn't magic. The latest research on how decisions are made tells us a lot about why Sun Tzu's principles work. It comes from using patterns to retrain our mind to see conditions differently. The study of successful response arose from military confrontations, where every battle clearly demonstrated how hard it is to predict events in the real world. Sun Tzu saw that winners were always those who knew how to respond appropriately to the dynamic nature of their situation.

Sun Tzu's principles provides a complete model for the key knowledge for understanding conditions in complex dynamic environments. This model "files" each piece of data into the appropriate place in the big picture. As the picture of your situation fills in, you can identify the opportunities hidden within your situation.

Making Decisions about Conditions

Instead of focusing on a series of planned steps, Sun Tzu's principles are about making decisions regarding conditions. It concerns itself with: 1) identifying the relative strengths and weaknesses of competitive positions, 2) advancing positions leveraging opportunities, and 3) the types of responses to specific challenges that work the most frequently. Using Sun Tzu's principles, we call these three areas position awareness , opportunity development , and situation response . Each area that we master broadens your capabilities.

- Position awareness trains us to recognize that competitive situations are defined by the relationship among alternative positions. Developing this perspective never ends. It deepens throughout our lives.
- Opportunity development explores the ground, testing our perceptions. Only testing the edges of perspective through action can we know what is true.
- S ituation response trains us to recognize the key characteristics of the immediate situation and to respond appropriately. Only by practice, can we learn to trust the viewpoint we have developed.

Success in competitive environments comes from making better decisions every day. Sharp strategic reflexes flow from a clear understanding of where and when you use which competitive tools methods.

The Key Viewpoints

As an individual, you have a unique and valuable viewpoint, but every viewpoint is inherently limited by its own position. The result is that people cannot get a useful perspective on their own situations and surrounding opportunities. The first formula of positioning awareness involve learning what information is relevant. The most advanced techniques teach how to gather that information and put it into a bigger picture.

Most people see their current situations as the sum of their past successes and failures. Too often people dwell on their mistakes while simultaneously sitting on their laurels. Sun Tzu's strategy forces you to see your position differently. How you arrived at your current position doesn't matter. Your position is what it is. It is shaped by history but history is not destiny.

In this framework, the only thing that matters is where you are going and how you are going to get there. As you begin to develop your strategic reflexes, you start to think more and more about how to secure your current position and advance it.

Seeing the Big Picture

Most people see all the details of their lives, but they cannot see what those detail mean in terms of the big picture. As you master position awareness, you don't see your life as a point but as a path. You see your position in terms of what is changing and what resources are available. You are more aware of your ability to make decisions and your skills in working with others.

Most importantly, this strategic system forces you to get in touch with your core set of goals and values.

Untrained people usually see their life in terms of absolutes: successes and failures, good luck and bad, weakness and strength. As you begin to master position awareness, you begin to see all comparisons of strength and weakness are temporary and relative. A position is not strong or weak in itself. Its strength or weakness depends on how it compares or "fits" with surrounding positions. Weakness and strength are not what a position is, but how you use it.

The Power of Perspective

Positional awareness gives you the specialized vocabulary you need to understanding how situations develop. Mastering this vocabulary, you begin to see the leverage points connecting past and future. You replace vague conceptions of "strength," "momentum," and "innovation" with much more pragmatic definitions that you can actually use on a day to day basis.

Mastering position awareness also changes your relationships with other people. It teaches you a different way of judging truth and character. This methods allow you to spot self-deception and dishonest in others. It also allows you to understand how you can best work with others to compensate for your different weaknesses.

Once you develop a good perspective of position, it naturally leads you to want to learn more about how you can improve you position through the various aspects of opportunity development covered in the subsequent parts of the Strategy Playbook.

Seeing the Invisible

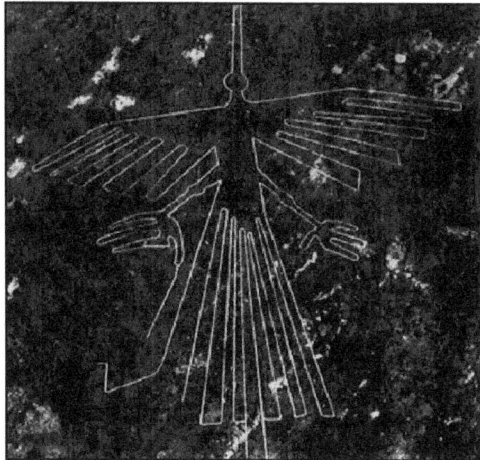

The "Nazca lines" are giant drawings etched across thirty miles of desert on Peru's southern coast. The patterns are only visible at a distance of hundreds of feet in the air. Below that, they look like strange paths or roads to nowhere. Just as we cannot see these lines without the proper perspective, people who master Sun Tzu's methods can <u>suddenly recognize situations</u> that were invisible to them before. Unless we have the right perspective, we cannot compare situations and positions successfully. The most recent scientific research explains why people cannot see these patterns for comparison without developing the network framework of adaptive thinking.[1]

Seeing Patterns

We can imagine patterns in chaotic situations, but seeing real pattern is the difference between success and failure. In our seminars, we demonstrate the power of seeing patterns in a number of exercises.

The <u>mental models</u> used by warrior give them "situation awareness." This situation awareness isn't just vague theory. Recent research shows that it can be measured in a variety of ways.[2] We now know that untrained people fall victim to a flow of confusing information because they don't know where its pieces fit. Those trained in Sun Tzu's mental models plug this stream of information quickly and easily into a bigger picture, transforming the skeleton's provided by Sun Tzu's system into a functioning awareness of your strategic position and its relation to other positions. Each piece of information has a place in that picture. As the information comes in, it fills in the picture, like pieces of a puzzle.

The ability to see the patterns in this bigger picture allows experts in strategy to see what is invisible to most people in a number of ways. They include:

- People trained in Art of War principles--<u>recognition-primed decision-making</u> --see patterns that others do not.
- Trained people can spot anomalies, things that should happen in the network of interactions but don't.
- Trained people are in touch with changes in the environment within appropriate time horizons.
- Trained people recognize complete patterns of interconnected elements under extreme time pressure.

Procedures Make Seeing Difficult

One of the most surprising discoveries from this research is that those who know procedures, that is, a linear view of events, alone have a ***more*** difficult time recognizing patterns than novices. An interesting study[3] examined the different recognition skills of three groups of people 1) experts, 2) novices, and 3) trainers who taught the standard procedures. The three groups were asked to pick out an expert from a group novices in a series of videos showing them performing a decision-making task, in this case, CPR. Experts were able to recognize the expert 90% of the time. Novices recognized the expert 50% of the time. The shocking fact was that trainers performed much worse that the novices, recognizing the expert only 30% of the time.

Why do those who know procedures fail to see what the experts usually see and even novices often see? Because, as research into <u>mental simulations</u> has shown, those with only a procedural model fit everything into that model and ignore elements that don't fit. In the above experiment, interviews with the trainers indicated that they assumed that the experts would always follow the procedural model. In real life, experts adapt to situations where unique conditions often trump procedure. Adapting to the situation rather than following set procedures is a central focus the form of strategy that the Institute teaches.

Missing Expected Elements

People trained to recognize the bigger picture beyond procedures also recognize when expected elements are missing from the picture. These anomalies or, what the cognition experts[4] describe as "negative cues" are invisible to novices *and* to those trained only in procedure. Without sense of the bigger pattern, people are focused too narrowly on the problem at hand. The "dog that didn't bark" from the Sherlock Holmes story, "Silver Blaze," is the most famous example of a negative cue. Only those working from a larger nonprocedural framework can expect certain things to happen and notice when they don't.

The ability to see what is missing also comes from the expectations generated by the mental model. Process-oriented models have the expectation of one step following another, but situation-recognition models create their expectations from signals in the environment. Research[5] into the time horizons of decision-makers shows that different time scales are at work. People at the highest level of organizations must look a year or two down the road, using strategic models that work in that timeframe, doing strategic planning. Decision-makers on the front-lines, however, have to react within minutes or even seconds to changes in their situation, working from their strategic reflexes. The biggest danger is that people get so wrapped up in a process that they lose contact with their environment.

Decisions Under Pressure

Extreme time pressure is what distinguishes front-line decision-making from strategic planners. One of the biggest discoveries in cognitive research[6] is that trained people do much better in seeing their situation instantly and making the correct decisions under time pressure. Researchers found virtually no difference between the decisions that experts made under time pressure when comparing them to decisions made without time pressure. That research also finds that those with less experience and training made dramatically worse decisions when they were put under time pressure.

The central argument for training our strategic reflexes is that our situation results, not from chance or luck, but from <u>the instant decisions</u> that that we all make every day. Our position is the sum of these decisions. If we cannot make the right decisions on the spot, when they are needed, our plans usually come to nothing. This is why we describe training people's strategic reflexes as helping them "do at first what most people only do at last."

The success people experience seeing what is invisible to others is dramatic. To learn more about how the strategic reflexes we teach differ from what can be planned, read about <u>the contrast between planning and reflexes here</u> . As <u>our many members report</u>, the success Sun Tzu's system makes possible is remarkable.

1 Chi, Glaser, & Farr, 1988, The Nature of Expertise, Erlbaum
2 Endsley & Garland, Analysis and Measurement of Situation Awareness
3 Klein & Klein, 1981, "Perceptual/Cognitive Analysis of proficient CPR Performance", Midwestern Psychological Association Meeting, Chicago.
4 Dr. David Noble, Evidence Based Research, Inc.In Gary Klein, Sources of Power, 1999
5 Jacobs & Jaques, 1991, "Executive Leadership".In Gal & Mangelsdofs (eds.), Handbook of Military Psychology, Wiley
6 Calder, Klein, Crandall,1988, "Time Pressure, Skill, and Move Quality in Chess". American Journal of Psychology, 101:481-493

1.0.0 Strategic Positioning

Sun Tzu's eight key methods defining competitive strategy in terms of developing relatively superior positions.

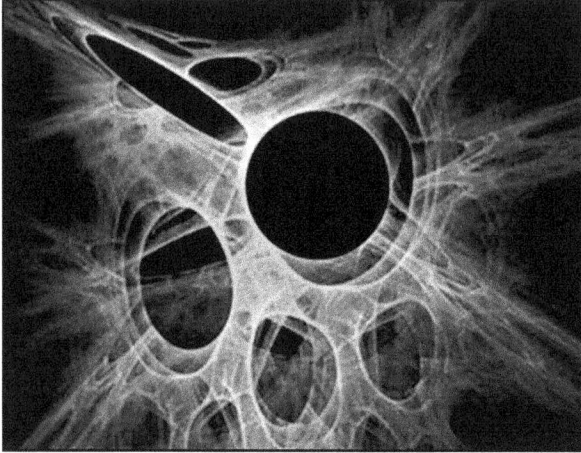

"Use your position as your war's centerpiece."
Sun Tzu's The Art of War 6:7:5

"When science finally locates the center of the universe, some people will be surprised to learn they're not it."
Bernard Bailey

General Principle: Strategy starts with understanding positioning.

Situation:

Sun Tzu's strategy explains the interactions of objects that we call positions. Like molecules or atomic particles, positions have various characteristics. We can analyze and compare positions and discuss how they "work" because we can discuss these general characteristics. While all positions may be a unique combination of characteristics, the characteristics themselves are not unique. Like all molecules consist of elemental atoms, all positions consist of elements that we can instantly recognize and evaluate. We can make decisions about the relative value and strength of various positions on the basis of these elements.

Opportunity:

Before Sun Tzu's *The Art of War,* success in competition was often explained solely by size. The rule was simple: the larger the force--whether an army or a single fighter, the more likely it was to win. The problem was that this rule did not explain what really happened in competitive situations where the smaller force often did win. It also didn't explain *how* some forces became larger than others. Sun Tzu saw that 1) size was not an advantage in many types of competitive situations, and 2) size itself could be explained by a more elemental concept, the idea of positioning. Positions with advantages create success easily. The size of an organization is a result of good positioning.

Sun Tzu's strategy defines the principles by which positions interact with other positions in the competitive environment. These principles are not deterministic, telling us what will always happen. Like the rules of subatomic physics, these rules are stochastic, that is, a matter of probabilities. These principles must also factor in our self-awareness and creativity. Unlike the interactions of subatomic particles which are naturally restricted to a finite set of reactions, we can consciously invent new reactions, reversing the expectations of others. This means probabilities are not fixed but constantly changing. However, all of these reactions are constrained by the basic nature of positions, which are defined by the following key methods.

Key Methods: The following eight key methods explain the basics of Sun Tzu's concept of strategic positions.

1. Competitive positions are paths. They are anchored in the past and have a direction toward a goal in the future (1.1 Position Paths).

2. Competitive positions have both objective and subjective characteristics. Competitive positions exist both in the external world and in the human mind. Both of these aspects of a position determine how competitive decisions are made (1.2 Subobjective Positions).

3. Competitive positions can be compared on five key components. Competitive positions are compared and interact with the competitive positions around them. These interactions take place in the competitive environment. Just as the environment of subatomic particles exists as other subatomic particles, the competitive environment is best viewed in terms of other strategic positions. The elements are mission, climate, ground, leader, and methods. Comparing these key areas are the basis of our competitive decision-making (1.3 Elemental Analysis).

4. The external competitive environment drives change and provides rewards. Without change, there would be no opportunities and without rewards, there would be no competition (1.4 The External Environment).

5. The internal capabilities of a competitor are determined solely from making decisions and executing them. We call these two internal components command and methods (1.5 Competing Agents).

6. All positions are built around a set of motivations that determine both direction and strength. This is the core of a strategic position (1.6 Mission Values).

7. Positions are advanced through an adaptive loop of continually adjusting responses to events. Events come from our external environment but our responses arise from our internal capabilities (1.8 Progress Cycle).

8. The skills of external competitive success are the opposite of those of internal production. The two skill sets are complementary opposites. However, both competitive and productive success depend upon each other (1.9 Competition and Production).

Illustration: These key methods of positioning govern every form of competition and every type of competitors. Each organization has a strategic position. The individuals that make up those organizations also each have their own strategic positions, both inside and outside of their organizations. We have positions in our personal relationships, in our career, in our social life, in our work-place, among our friends, and so on. Sports teams, military units, politicians, product brands, salespeople, negotiators, lawyers and every other profession in a competitive arena are actually working with competitive positions.

All of these positions are governed by the same eight key methods. As an application of these key methods, let's simply apply them to a career.

1. Competitive positions are paths. We can get jobs that our past jobs qualify us for and which take us toward our career goals. This is our career path.

2. Competitive positions have both objective and subjective characteristics. Our career path is determined both by our actual performance and how that performance is perceived by others. These two aspects of the job are related but they can be very different.

3. Competitive positions can be compared on five key components. Our career is judged by our career goals and values, job market changes, our current employer and industry, our decision-making skills, and our skill at performing our job.

4. The external competitive environment drives change and provides rewards. We can control neither industry trends nor how people are paid within our profession or industry.

5. The internal characteristics of a position determine its capabilities. We can develop our decision-making skills and our professional knowledge and abilities.

6. All positions are built around a set of motivations that determine both their direction and strength. We must balance our career choices depending on the relative importance of money, time with family, job risk, job stress, job satisfaction, and so on.

*7. **Positions are advanced through an adaptive loop of continually adjusting responses to events.*** Getting raises, promotions and a better position at another company are all based on the same adaptive process.

8. T*he skills of external competitive success are the opposite of those used in internal productive success.* Competition focuses on adapting to people while production focuses performing tasks. Getting a promotion to a new position requires different skills than performing well in that position. Our ability to demonstrate our expanded abilities depends on getting promotions, but how well we perform determines our ability to get the next promotion.

1.1.0 Position Paths

Sun Tzu's six key methods defining the continuity of strategic positions over time.

"Use an indirect route as your highway.
Use the search for advantage to guide you."
                              Sun Tzu's The Art of War 7:1:9

"You cannot travel the path until you have become the path itself."
                              Gautama Siddharta

General Principle: Strategy requires predicting the direction of strategic positions.

Situation:

Positions rise and fall over time. The direction of strategic positions is affected both by conditions in the environment and the decisions that people in those positions make and act upon. Positions not only follow paths, rising and falling over time, but strategic positions are those paths. Their past and direction are critical parts of what they are and how they must be understood.

The problem is that positions change so slowly and gradually that we cannot see those changes easily. In our everyday lives, we often think of positions as static resting places. In everyday terms, we describe a person's "position" in a static way as part of a social hierarchy or as a clearly defined role in an organization or institution. This person is a department manager. That person is a priest or a lawyer. This is not the way we think about positions when we analyze strategic environments. We always attempt to look at positions not only in terms of where they are right now, but where they have come from and where they are going.

Opportunity:

The Chinese character that we translate as "mission" is *tao*. *Tao* literally means the "way" and the "path." Our method for using positions depends on understanding both their nature, their history, and their purpose. A strategic position is different from molecules or atomic particles because we are aware of our positions. Positions are created and directed by conscious beings not inanimate objects. We have come from somewhere in the past. Not only do we remember that past, but everyone in our environment remembers it as well. Our histories are part of our position, directing to some degree where we can go in the future. Strategic positions are always under someone's conscious control. This means that their direction is not random. It can be changed at any time by the choices and actions of those directing them. Positions have a direction because we care about our mission, that is, our goals and values. We make decisions to move toward our goals. We move into the future while making choices that shape the future.

Key Methods:

The following six key methods describe how we think about positions as paths.

*1. **Strategic positions are dynamic.*** The positions are temporary, a snapshot in time. What is harder to see is that positions are always changing, rising or falling, waxing or waning (1.1.1 Position Dynamics).

*2. **Strategic positions have persistence.*** People always defend their existing positions because we are all anchored to our past. Our histories are part of what we are and what we defend (1.1.2 Defending Positions).

*3. **Change is a key part of both the objective and subjective aspects of a position.*** In quantum mechanics and Sun Tzu's strategy, the concept of "at rest" doesn't even exist. All positions always have both speed and direction and our perception of that speed and direction shapes our decisions (1.2 Subobjective Positions).

4. *Our decisions must be based on our view of the motion of position paths in our environment.* All the strategic decisions that we make are executed in the future. We must make these decisions based upon where positions are in that future, not where they are now (1.4 The External Environment).

*5. **If we understand people's histories and motivations, we can approximate future position paths.*** This requires knowing our Art of War principles, what others have done in the past, and their specific goals (1.5.2. Group Methods).

*6. **As paths, future strategic positions are impossible to predict exactly.*** Unlike the paths of subatomic particles or baseballs, strategic paths are constantly changing because we are constantly learning. That learning affects the future vector of our positions. Skills are acquired and certain attitudes are formed. Mark Twain once described an education as the path from "cocky ignorance to miserable uncertainty." While learning our Art of War principles makes us keenly aware of what we cannot know, it also assures us that we will know more than those around us. Since these paths are under conscious control, their direction can be changed at any time (1.5.1 Command Leadership).

Illustration:

In sports, players must not think about where the ball is but where the ball will be. This is an extremely useful analogy for understanding the nature of strategic positions.

1. Strategic positions are dynamic. Both players and the ball move. The strategic situation is the changing configuration of the players' and the balls' positions.

2. Strategic positions have persistence. The goal posts do not move. Players have certain skills, reputations, and tendencies based upon their past experience.

3. Change is a key part of both the objective and subjective aspects of a position. A player acts based not only upon what the other players do but upon what he or she thinks they will do. Of course, players know that the other players have certain expectations about their behavior and they adapt their behavior based on that knowledge.

4. Our decisions must be based on our view of the motion of position paths in our environment. We do not play to where the ball and the other players are, we play according to where we think they will be.

5. If we understand people's histories and motivations, we can approximate future position paths. Even though we cannot know exactly what will happen when a player touches the ball, we can guess because we know the rules and goal of the game. The better we know the habits and skills of the player, the more accurate our prediction. The same is true of strategy.

6. As paths, future strategic positions are impossible to predict exactly. In sports, the path of a ball is relatively easy to calculate until a player touches it. After it is launched and before it is touched, the ball's path is controlled solely by the predictable laws of physics. Once a player touches it, however, all predictions are off. The balls future path cannot be predicted because its future path is controlled by the intentions and skill of the player.

1.1.1 Position Dynamics

Sun Tzu's seven key methods defining how all current positions are always getting better or worse.

"Positions turn around.
Nevertheless, you must never be defeated."
Sun Tzu's The Art of War 5:4:5

"Don't take life too seriously. It's only a temporary condition."

Bill Knapp

General Principle: All current strategic positions are temporary.

Situation: Since Sun Tzu teaches that all strategic positions are paths, we must see all current strategic positions as dynamic. While this sounds exciting, it really means that all positions are temporary. The temporary nature of strategic positions is a problem. It means that, given bad choices or just inactivity, our positions will naturally decline over time. It is easy to take our positions for granted.

As unpredicted events arise that seem to help or hurt our position, it is easy to make the mistake of thinking that our position depends on luck. The problem is that we think of these events as good or bad in themselves. We do not want to admit that our decisions put us in the path of these events. We do not want to admit that our response to every event is more important than the event itself.

Opportunity:

The temporary nature of positions also means that, given good decisions, positions can and do improve over time. Indeed, most of us generally improve our positions throughout our lives until age catches up with us. Most of us do this without knowing Sun Tzu's strategy. Our environment naturally provides both incentives and opportunities to improve positions. Even without a deep understanding of strategic positions, most of us improve our position if only because most of those we compete with also lack a deep understanding of strategic positions. It is our recognition of the opportunities in certain situations and our decisions to take advantage of them, not the situations themselves, that are the deciding factor in how our positions change. Our current position is always just the starting point. Our future paths are made possible by the conditions in our environment but it is determined by our skill at making decisions every day.

Key Methods:

To recognize and take advantage of situations, we must see them as a constellation of potential positions using the following seven key methods of Sun Tzu.

1. Shifting environmental conditions and our actions change our position. Our position changes automatically because conditions in the environment are always changing. As others around us act, their shifts of position affect our own because all positions are relative. As we prepare for events and respond to them, our own actions shift our positions and the relationships with others. Our environment and our reactions to it create constant elemental change (1.3 Elemental Analysis).

2. Our position changes even if we do nothing. We cannot stop the changes of nature and the actions of others. Sometimes these changes will improve our position, but more often, if we do nothing, our position changes for the worst. Strategy always involves making decisions about timing to adjust to this change. Change is built into our position because climate is always changing (1.4.1 Climate Shift).

3. The most predictable of all changing conditions is aging. We can predict with 100% certainty that all of us will one year older a year from now or dead, no exceptions. Aging can be many things. There is a difference between ten years of experience and one year of experience repeated ten times. Our use of aging determines the path of each individual's position. Our strategic position naturally improves after we are born because as we mature, we develop more abilities and more skills. After we physically mature, we enter into a long plateau where our aging has a much smaller affect on our position. However, toward the end of our lives, our abilities naturally begin to decline over time. Time limitations are built into everything (3.1.6 Time Limitations).

4. Every position loses its capability over time by consuming its limited resources. Everything ages. If not maintained and built up, every object that we build decays with time. This pattern of decay includes strategic positions, which are human constructs. The resources of every position are limited. If we use them without adding to them, the position loses its capabilities to support itself (3.1.1 Resource Limitations).

5. Supporters change their decisions about our position over time. Our existing positions are established based on the past choices by our supporters. When our supporters change their opinions about us, those changes undermine the positions that we have based on their support. Even without dramatic shifts in climate that necessitate re-evaluating their support, people eventually crave novelty. While people tend to continue doing what they have done in the past, they eventually make different choices (2.3.1 Action and Reaction).

6. Unless we improve our positions over time, they will naturally tend to decay. In Sun Tzu's vision, there is a natural balance in the universe that swings from fullness to emptiness. Aging, running out of resources and losing support are all symptomatic of this greater truth of balancing complementary opposites (3.5 Strength and Weakness).

7. ***Over time, the cumulative effects of our decisions have a greater impact on our positions.*** People are constantly acting to change their positions. The difference between levels of success has less to do with accidents of environmental conditions than the quality of the choices that people make on a day-to-day basis. Of course, the purpose of Sun Tzu's strategy is to explain how this is most easily accomplished in what we call the Progress Cycle (1.8 Progress Cycle).

Illustration:

Let us examine these principles by comparing them to a book by Malcolm Gladwell, called ***Outliers***, that makes the argument that success depends primarily on fortuitous environmental conditions beyond our control. His examples are the careers of people such as Bill Gates.

1. ***Shifting environmental conditions and our actions change our position.*** As Gladwell explains, Bill Gates was fortunate to find himself in a private high school with access to one of the first timeshare computers, enabling him to learn a technology unavailable to almost everyone else. This fallacious viewpoint focuses on the unusual, outlier successes like that of Gates. This hypothesis selectively filters out the typical success stories that are all around us. Drive down any business district in any town in America and the majority of the businesses that you see are not part of large corporations like Microsoft, but small businesses, started and built by individuals over the course of their lifetimes. These typical success stories built up their positions over time. These are the people that go on to become the "millionaire next door." For every Bill Gates, there are literally millions of these successes all over the world. Since all of these people are financially independent, the fact that they are not wealthy on the scale of a Bill Gates does not degrade their success.

2. ***Our position changes even if we do nothing.*** Forgetting all the decisions that led Gates from that school into the software busi-

ness, there were hundreds of other bright kids in that school with Bill Gates who had access to those same time-share computers. None of them went on to start leading software companies. Indeed, a few of those children, despite their advantages, almost certainly became alcoholics and drug addicts. Some of their positions ended up worse than those of their parents.

3. ***The most predictable of all changing conditions is aging.*** Like many "outlier" success stories, Bill Gates found his success early in life. This is not true for the average, everyday success story where most people's ability to earn increases throughout their lives as their capabilities increase. Even as their earning capability declines, most older people have accumulated many times the wealth of younger people simply because of aging.

4. ***Every position loses its capability over time by consuming its limited resources.*** The company that Bill Gates started, Microsoft, is completely different today than it was when Gates first made his fortunes. Had it kept selling its first product, the BASIC programming language for 8-bit microprocessors, it would have disappeared long ago. It was the subsequent positions of Windows, MS-Office, and other products that kept Bill Gates in his position as one of the most successful people in the world. Had his organization stayed in any of its early positions, it would have disappeared as certainly as Visicalc, DEC and Compaq, once the most dominating companies in their field.

5. ***Supporters change their decisions about our position over time.*** The untypical success of Bill Gates and typical success of the millions of millionaires-next-door have one thing in common: they are able to maintain their base of support over time. Millionaires cannot force customers and others to deal with them. Every day, those customers must be won anew.

6. ***Unless we improve our positions over time, they will naturally tend to decay.*** Many of the choices that people make can, of course, damage their position. Dropping out of school, using drugs and alcohol, not getting married, divorce, early pregnancy, a preference for self-indulgent activities, i.e. pleasing yourself, over productive activities, i.e. pleasing others etc. All of our choices have a predictable negative impact on our positions over time. While someone who makes bad choices can get lucky and win the lottery, these chance changes have surprisingly little effect on his/her position over time. Virtually all people who are in bad positions because of making bad choices quickly find themselves back in a bad position no matter how lucky they are.

Over time, the cumulative effects of our decisions have a greater impact on our positions. It was Bill's decisions that made the difference in the course of his life. Those decisions determined his position today as the world's richest man. Of course, one's actions are not guaranteed to advance a position.

1.1.2 Defending Positions

Sun Tzu's six key methods defining the basic ways that we defend our current positions until new positions are established.

*"You are sometimes unable to win.
You must then defend."*

Sun Tzu's The Art of War 4:2:2-3

"If you are not prepared to use force to defend civilization, then be prepared to accept barbarism."

Thomas Sowell

General Principle: Current positions must be defended until new positions are established.

Situation: At its heart, Sun Tzu's strategy is based on simple economics. We get resources from our current position. We can use these resources to defend our position, advance, or extend it. These resources are limited. We must make choices about how we use them. The problem is that we can only advance our position when an opportunity presents itself. Until we discover that opportunity, we must maintain our existing position. We need our position because opportunities arise from our environment within the reach of our existing position. If we do not protect our existing position, opportunities cannot come knocking. Everything that has been part of our position in the past need not be defended forever, but we must always defend the parts of our position that touch on future opportunities.

Opportunity:

The more ground our positions control, the more resources we can access to advance our position. However, the more ground we control, the more resources we need to protect and maintain those resources. Defending positions competes for resources with advancing a position, but if we fail to defend our position, we lose resources and the connections needed to advance position. As the source of all our resources except for time, the ground that we control determines many of our basic capabilities (1.3.2 Element Scalability). The minimal ground that we can control is our own body. The minimal climate is our own attitudes and time. We extend our position by controlling more ground. We must defend our existing ground to hold onto our existing resources in order to have the resources to extend our position.

Key Methods:

Like so much in using Sun Tzu's principles, we are looking for the right balance. We need just enough defense, not too much or too little as expressed in these six key methods.

1. We know what we need to defend and what we do not need to defend. This means knowing what is worth defending. The basic standard is that we must defend the aspects of our ground that generate the most resources for the least effort and the most opportunities for the future (9.2 Points of Vulnerability).

2. We must avoid doing too little to defend our existing position. This usually means taking certain aspects of our position for granted. The most common mistake is taking our current position (and its resources) for granted. As we explained in the last post, positions naturally decay over time. If we are not maintaining that position, it can weaken to the point that its suddenly breaks. We can visualize an under-defended section of a position if we think of positions as a path. Imagine just a part of that path is weakening, growing thinner, and more fragile. If that part of the position is unimportant and unnecessary, outliving its value, this does not matter, but if that link ties together key parts of our current position, its loss can be devastating. In our practical wisdom, we recognize that a chain is only as strong as its weakest link (5.6.1 Defense Priority).

3. We must avoid defending every aspect of our position all the time. Being too defensive consumes valuable resources and creates strategic weakness. The other most common mistake is the opposite of the first: developing a defensive posture where we try to defend everything that has ever been part of our position all the time. The most extreme form of this defensive posture is a state of paranoia. This state of mind, while it is certainly defensive, can actually destroy the position that it seeks to defend. People that are too defensive find it impossible to let go of anything, especially the past. The position that they maintain (at least in their own minds) trails so far back into the past that it becomes a drag on moving forward. When we defend areas that do not require defending, we eat up the resources we need to advance our position (3.1.1 Resource Limitations).

4. We must see positions as stepping stones. In moving forward, we must sometimes leave things behind. However, we never give up all aspects of our current position. We never want to start developing a position over from scratch. Again, the key is balance. We must defend our existing position to get any opportunity to advance it. We must not defend it to such a degree that we destroy it or our opportunities to advance in the future (1.1.1 Position Dynamics).

5. We must move into new positions quickly but out of existing positions slowly. If a strategic position was a single point, this wouldn't be possible. A point cannot be in two places at once. However, since positions are a path, we always have a position to defend even when we are advancing to a new position (1.1 Position Paths).

6. We must avoid stretching ourselves too thin without abandoning the past. In these situations, we want to maintain and defend everything that is valuable in our existing position. Everything is a potential source of new opportunities (4.6.1 Spread-Out Conditions).

Illustration:

Let us illustrate these key methods with a variety of examples.

1. We know what we need to defend and what we do not need to defend. Our job, our current relationships, any assets that we control (money, house, car, etc). all represent parts of our position that we must defend. Certain aspects of our position consist of material property that we can use, but our resources also include all of the relationships that we have with other people. Everything everyone knows about us, that is, our reputation, is a part of our position. In strategic terms, fame is seen simply as an extension of position into more people's minds.

2. We must avoid doing too little to defend our existing position. For example, people's marriages get into trouble simply because they take them for granted and do not continue to work to defend them. They make the mistake of either taking their marriage for granted or thinking of a spouse as easily replaced. In fact, one of the most common keys to success is having a stable marriage. Divorce is a consistent predictors of failure because it indicates the inability to recognize what is valuable and defend it.

3. We must avoid defending every aspect of our position all the time. Think about Bogart's character of Commander Queeg in the movie, *The Caine Mutiny*. It was his concern about protecting his position that lead to its destruction. Maintaining positions requires maintaining relationships and nothing destroys relationships faster than exhibiting a lack of trust to those around us.

4. We must see positions as stepping stones. For example, to take a new job, we must usually leave our old one. When we mount steps, one foot must support our weight in the past while the other foot moves forward. Even when we take a new job, we bring as many skills, contacts, and resources with us from the old one as we can.

5. *We must move into new positions quickly but out of existing positions slowly.* For example, if we want to start our own home business, we can do so immediately but do it while maintaining our regular employment. We only quit our job when the home business has grown big enough to support us.

6. *We must avoid stretching ourselves too thin without abandoning the past.* For example in a business, we can add new customers and products without abandoning old ones.

1.2 Subobjective Positions

Sun Tzu's nine key methods describing the subjective and objective aspects of a position.

"When you are ready, you appear incapacitated.
When active, you pretend inactivity.
When you are close to the enemy, you appear distant.
When far away, you appear near. "

Sun Tzu's The Art of War 1:4:3-6

"More important than innate disposition, objective
experience, and environment is the subjective evaluation

of these. Furthermore, this evaluation stands in a certain, often strange, relation to reality."

Alfred Adler

General Principle: Strategic landscapes and positions are neither objective or subjective but join aspects of both.

Situation:

Strategic positions on competitive landscapes exist in two planes at once. They exist both in the physical universe and in our minds. We say that they are "subobjective," simultaneously subjective and objective, consisting of both facts and opinions. This dual nature of positions and their competitive landscape is essential to understanding strategic positions. We can never know the complete objective truth about any situation. We can know facts, but the meaning of facts are filtered through our opinions of what those facts mean. We have our subjective perceptions, which capture a part of that truth filtered through our mental models.

Opportunity:

While there is only one objective reality, every one of us has a unique subjective perspective on that position. The gap between perception and reality can create opportunities (3.6 Leveraging Subjectivity). Very different perspectives on a situation give us different insights into the underlying, essentially unknowable, objective reality. Discovering the overlooked openings in that reality are the basis of all opportunity (3.1.4 Openings).

In an information economy, more and more people work with information and systems. and they are more disconnected from the underlying realities on which that information is based. This creates an opportunity for those who are closer to the underlying objective reality of a situation. The feedback loops connecting people to those underlying realities become longer, allowing greater deviations from reality over time (3.4.3 Reaction Lag). Larger organizations are especially vulnerable in this area (3.4 Dis-Economies of Scale). The larger they are, the greater the disconnect between objective and subjective aspects of their positions. This weakness is an opportunity for their competitors.

Key Methods:

Since we do not have complete information, we use the following nine key methods to improve our subjective judgments about positions.

1. We accept that we cannot know objective reality no matter how much information we have. There will always be a gap in our assessment of reality. The complexity of competitive situations is a potential trap for decision-making because we can always delay our decisions. There is always more information to be gathered (3.6 Leveraging Subjectivity).

2. We all have incentives to view and portray situations to our advantage. Sometimes this is intentional deception, but often it is self-deception as well. This fact tends to create more distance between objective reality and the subjective opinions that people hold about that reality (2.1.3 Strategic Deception).

3. The objective and subjective aspects of a position are "complementary opposites." This means that they are intimately joined and create one another in a loop. Each aspect of the dynamic shapes the other. Correctly understood, reality and opinion are not two separate things, but one thing with two components in dynamic balance (3.2.3 Complementary Opposites).

4. All subjective opinions are not equally close to their underlying reality. Some perspectives are very close to reality while other perspectives are total nonsense. (4.4 Strategic Distance).

5. Very different perspectives can be equally close to the underlying reality. Niels Bohr said that the opposite of a correct statement is a false statement, but the opposite of a profound truth may well be another profound truth. It is our breadth of perspective on a situation that allows us to see it with more clarity, especially in terms of understanding the forces shaping them (2.5 The Big Picture).

6. We must expect a larger gap between reality and perception when our information is older. It takes time to gather information. As we gather information, the situation is changing. The older our information, the more the situation has changed (1.1.1 Position Dynamics).

7. When stretched too far, events will snap subjective opinions back closer to reality. The further opinion stretches from reality, the greater the tension and instability of the situation. Opinion can snap back to reality almost instantly as events confront us with our foolishness (3.2.5 Dynamic Reversal).

8. Because of the subjective nature of our opinions, we test our perceptions against objective reality as soon as possible. We need to see the effects of our decisions on events. We want mistakes in our subjective judgments to be quickly corrected by events (1.8.3 Cycle Time).

9. Since reality is different than our opinions, we adapt our subjective views to better fit new information. This creates a constant loop between the objective and subjective nature of strategic positions. Our subjective view of positions changes the objective reality by guiding our actions. We run into problems when we cling to our subjective view when we get objective information that contradicts it. The objective reality of a position should change our subjective view when we observe an event inconsistent with our subjective view (1.8.2 The Adaptive Loop).

Illustration:

The gap between objective and subjective positions explains the financial/economic crisis of 2008-2009 that began with the world-wide distribution of bad real estate loans.

1. We accept that we cannot know objective reality no matter how much information we have. The objective reality of individual mortgage loans was relatively simple, but those loans were bundled to create complexity. On the objective level of reality, specific pieces of property were mortgaged to specific people who had a specific ability to repay these loans. The banks making those loans, who were closer to their true quality or lack thereof, were forced into these many questionable loans by the government edicts of the Community Redevelopment Act. However, they also knew that they could sell off those loans to government organizations such as Fanny Mae and Freddy Mac despite their underlying soundness. Though their immediate perception of the loans based on the property and people involved may have been that they were bad, that subjective judgment was mitigated by the implicit government guarantee.

2. We all have incentives to view and portray situations to our advantage. Those loans were sold, bundled, and "repackaged" by organizations such as Fanny, Freddy, and later on Bear Stearns to be sold as financial investments. In doing so, their subjective positions were enhanced, creating more distance between the subjective and objective reality. Organizations such as Standard and Poors and Moody were brought in to give their imprimatur of approval to these investments. This improves their value in subjective measure in people's opinions, making money in the process. Organizations such as AIG were brought in to insure these investments, improving their subjective worth, and making money in the process. These organizations gave plenty of money to the politicians who, specifically those like Chris Dodd and Barney Franks, who in turn, gave their blessing to the process and protected it from investigation.

3. The objective and subjective aspects of a position are "complementary opposites." These loan packages were both the investments that were sold by the investment banks and the individual investments by real people in individual pieces of property. Both aspects were different sides of the same things. Their difference was in the side we happened to be looking at. Investors were shown one side. Only those deep within these organizations knew about the real loans to real people and their performance.

4. *All subjective opinions are not equally close to their underlying reality.* One of the great delusions of the linear thinking of organizational age (discussed in several free articles starting here) is that objective reality can be completely reflected in our reporting

systems. As someone who built an accounting software company, I am keenly aware of what can and cannot be captured by general accounting procedures. While financial reporting and other forms of reporting such as the balanced score card seek to create the illusion that objective reality can be completely captured and analyzed, the series study of strategic science is based on the sure knowledge that no reporting system can ever capture all relevant information. We cannot treat information as anything but a limited subjective perspective on the situation.

5. *Very different perspectives can be equally close to the underlying reality*. There was a huge difference between the view of those investing in these loan bundles and the views of those selling them. This was reflected by Goldman Sachs shorting these investments at the same time that it was selling them to customers.

6. *We must expect a larger gap between reality and perception when our information is older.* It took almost ten years for the reality to catch up to the fiction. Bad loans were being made because the government required bad loans to be main. However, since those loans were being sold with an implicit government guarantee, it took a long time for rising rates of mortgage defaults to catch up to the subjective reality.

7. *When stretched too far, events will snap subjective opinions back closer to reality.* However, the loop will always complete itself. In the end, the objective reality of what those loans were truly worth caught up with the high flying subjective vision created by the institutional process. The crash was sudden, but the U.S. government came through, pouring hundreds of billions of taxpayer dollars into hiding the problem. The day of reckoning was pushed into the future again in the form of inflation potential and loan burdens.

8. *Because of the subjective nature of our opinions, we test our perceptions against objective reality as soon as possible.* Disconnect between the objective and subjective nature of investments can not grow unless the government enables these errors. One way that they do this is though guarantees insuring investments whose value is too complex to be understood.

9. *Since reality is different than our opinions, we adapt our subjective views to better fit new information*. This is the big problem with bureaucracies enabled by laws. Laws such as the Community Reinvestment Act lock in views of reality that cannot be adapted. So, people adapt to the law rather than the reality. This creates one crisis after another, but government is not deterred. It sees each crisis as proof of the need for more laws and less individual freedom that allows people to easily adapt.

1.2.1 Competitive Landscapes

Sun Tzu's seven key methods regarding the arenas in which rivals jockey for position.

"Some commanders are not skilled in making adjustments to find an advantage. They can know the shape of the terrain.
Still, they cannot exploit the opportunities of their ground."

Sun Tzu's The Art of War 8:1:16-18

"The real voyage of discovery consists not in seeking new landscapes but in having new eyes."

Marcel Proust

"It is only in appearance that time is a river. It is rather a vast landscape and it is the eye of the beholder that moves."

Thornton Wilder

General Principle: Competitive landscapes are alive, complex and continually changing requiring constant adjustments.

Situation:

When we think of "landscape," we think of the mountains and lakes that are fixed and stable. The problem is that competitive landscapes are made of living people who are constantly moving. These complex landscapes are continually forming and reforming. Sun Tzu taught that our positions are intimately connecting to these "dancing" landscapes of competition. In the modern world, we are raised at home and school where the relationships are well-defined, stable, and simple. We grow up poorly prepared for finding our way on the dancing landscapes of competition. The world in which we find success in is not only competitive and complex but growing more and more competitive and complex every day.

Opportunity:

The complex nature of the competitive landscape requires a different way of seeing positions (1.2.3 Position Complexity). Because our positions arise from our interaction with others, competitive landscapes are filled with novelty and opportunity. Because everyone who makes up the landscape is adapting to everyone else, these competitive landscapes are surprisingly robust. The adaptive agents in complex environments adjust to changes. When a competitor fails, another takes his or her place. The balance within the network assures that any holes are filled automatically by those looking for a new advantage.

Key Methods:

The following seven key methods define the unique nature of competitive landscapes.

1. A competitive landscape defines the space in which competitive positions exist. This space is defined by the relations of both competitors and various resources within a larger environment. The competitive landscape consists of both physical and intellectual components. It is both objective and subjective in its shape, existing both in the physical world and in our mental models of that world (1.2 Subobjective Positions).

2. The area of a landscape consists of the total number of potential combinations of its elements. These various combinations of elements are described as the niches in the environment. These elements exist in both competitors and their environments. The match between the competitor and the environment measures a competitor's "fitness." Competitive landscapes are also known as fitness landscapes. Each element has a range of possible characteristics within it. These characteristics interact in a huge number of combinatorial possibilities. Each of these combinations defines a different potential position in the competitive landscape. Sun Tzu's strategy analyzes these elements and their characteristics to compare various positions (1.3 Elemental Analysis).

3. Advantage in the competitive landscape is the superior fitness of a given position. A better position better serves our goals. The shapes of the landscape are infinite because every competitor has a infinite set of changing goals. It is also finite because the basic resources that are required for survival are limited. The basic goals of survival are shared by everyone in the environment. Others types of goals are shared by smaller numbers of competitors within the competitive environment. (1.6 Mission Values).

4. Competitive landscapes are inherently rugged, having many different local peaks within them. The various combination of characteristics within the environment create different forms of superiority. Those different forms of superiority combine with the different desires of various competitors to create diverse value points in terrain. Different combinations of characteristics offer different costs and benefits, creating many different types of local peak positions (1.6.2 Types of Motivations).

5. Competitors continually reshape competitive landscapes as they interact and adapt. This means that the competitive landscape is dynamic, constantly changing. Competitors are interdependent. As competitors move within them seeking advantages, the landscape itself is reformed, affecting the shape of the terrain for other competitors. This reformation changes the relative advantages in existing positions and opens up entirely new areas for exploration. This reshaping exists both in our subjective perceptions and in objective realities that create competitive landscapes. It arises from the new types of resources and new combinations of resources that are discovered and utilized by various competitors (1.1.1 Position Dynamics).

*6. **Good strategy improves our position within the local landscape moving us into more advanced positions.*** Our actions primarily affect our position in the landscape but they can also move us into landscapes that better suit our mission. Strategy explores the competitive landscape, trying to identify directions for improving our position (5.2 Opportunity Exploration).

*7. **External competitive landscapes are much more complex than internal controlled environments.*** Competitive environments are shaped by adaptive interactions of independent actors. Controlled environments are shaped for a given purpose, designed to limit interactions among actors. While no environment can be perfectly controlled for long spans of time, there is a huge difference in complexity between the two environments. This difference in degree creates a difference in kind. Beyond a certain level of complexity, environments go through a phase transition. The rules that work within relatively simple, controlled environments, i.e. the rules of production, no longer work. Instead, what works are the key methods of competition, the principles of adaptive strategy (1.9 Competition and Production).

Illustration:

Let us apply these principles to define a marketplace.

*1. **A competitive landscape defines the space in which competitive positions exist.*** Products, customers, and suppliers all hold positions within the marketplace. The positions of these elements consist of both objective facts and subjective opinions about each of these elements.

*2. **The area of a landscape consists of the total number of potential combinations of its elements.*** This includes characteristics of customers, suppliers, and products and emergent properties such as the climate of the marketplace.

3. *Advantage in the competitive landscape is the superior fitness of a given position.* In marketplaces, market share is one measure of fitness. Profitability is another.

4. *Competitive landscapes are inherently rugged, having many different local peaks within them.* Many different types of product characteristics meet many different facets of customer needs. Subjectively, the best product for a given customer may not be the most popular or profitable. Objectively, we can compare products meeting similar needs on the number of customers they satisfy.

5. *Competitors continually reshape competitive landscapes as they interact and adapt.* Marketplaces for specific product categories grow and shrink over time. Within a marketplace, different products rise and fall. The creation of markets and the rise and fall of products within them are based upon the decisions actors make in regard to the changing situation.

6. *Good strategy improves our position within the local landscape moving us into more advanced positions.* The goal of most products is to increase their popularity and profitability. There are dominant positions within weak markets and more profitable ones. Competitors try to improve their products position within a market, find broader markets, and move to more profitable markets over time.

7. *External competitive landscapes are much more complex than internal controlled environments.* The marketplace in which products are sold is much more complex than the factories in which products are made.

1.2.2 Exploiting Exploration

Sun Tzu's seven key methods on how competitive landscapes are searched and positions utilized.

"You must use the philosophy of an invader.
Invade deeply and then concentrate your forces."
Sun Tzu's The Art of War 11:3:1-2

"As mankind continues to explore and exploit the
realm of space there needs to be some accounting and
understanding of the medium. Space is a new realm to
the human experience. "

Bruce Bookout

General Principle: Progress requires both searching for new positions and harvesting existing ones.

Situation:

Each of us has a strategic position, but few of us understand clearly how positions are acquired and developed by crossing boundaries. Our educational system teaches us methods for using the resources within the boundaries of our control. These skills teach us very little about how to explore competitive landscapes outside of those borders. "Exploitation" is an interesting word, meaning both "to use" and "to misuse," "to develop" and "to corrupt". This confusion about exploitation comes from our confusion about boundaries.

Opportunity:

Sun Tzu simplified competitive strategy by developing the idea of positions and boundaries. Boundaries limit our position. Positions can only be advanced by crossing boundaries. When we exploit resources with our control, exploitation is productive. When we exploit resources outside of our control, it becomes destructive. As with all of Sun Tzu's concepts, exploring the competitive landscape for resources and exploiting the resources discovered are complementary opposites. We cannot have one without the other.

Sometimes we must make the most of our existing position through exploitation (8.3.4 Position Production). At other times, we must expand or advance our position through exploration (5.2 Opportunity Exploration). Human happiness depends both upon being productive and upon constantly improving our situation.

Key Methods:

We use the following key methods to balance exploring the competitive landscape with exploiting our position.

1. Exploitation satisfies our immediate needs while exploration satisfies future needs. Exploiting our current position seeks to get the most immediate benefits from our current situation. Exploration seeks to maximize the benefits available from our future situation. Exploration is a gift that our current selves give to our future selves by creating progress in our lives. Satisfaction cannot come only come from being happy with what we have. Research shows that the source of happiness is earned success. In Sun Tzu's terms, this means that constantly improving our situation is the source of happiness (1.8 Progress Cycle).

2. Exploration of the competitive landscape requires adapting thinking and strategy. Exploration is a systematic search of the competitive landscape for better positions. Sun Tzu's strategy exists because some methods have been proven to work better at doing this than others. Exploration includes both finding better positions and gaining control of them for exploitation. During exploration, we must make decisions about mysterious areas. We decide which areas are worth exploring further and which are worth exploiting (1.9.1 Production Comparisons).

3. Exploitation of the competitive positions requires linear thinking and planning. Exploitation utilizes the resources of a specific position on the competitive landscape to generate value. Exploitation includes both developing and executing methods for harvesting the value from a given position. During exploitation, we increase our control over our position, maximizing its production of value. We usually discuss exploitation in terms of "production" and "management" (1.9.2 Span of Control).

4. We must strike a balance between exploration and exploitation. If we are constantly exploring the landscape, we never get any value from it. If we never explore new territory, we can only maximize the value of our current position. This process reaches a point of diminishing returns. Without exploration, we cannot advance our position by expanding or moving into richer areas on the competitive landscape. The methods of competition and production sustain each other (1.9 Competition and Production).

5. Positions are exploited and landscapes explored on both subjective and objective planes. We explore the objective and subjective aspects of competitive landscapes looking for opportunities to improve our position. Opportunities to improve our position can exist in the physical nature of our environment, the opinions of other people, or in the gap between the objective reality and subjective opinion (1.2 Subobjective Positions).

6. The relative advantages of positions for exploitation are constantly changing in the competitive landscape. Dynamics are built into the competitive landscape. Change occurs both on the subjective and objective planes. The nature of superiority changes as our individual needs and goals shift over time. The relative advantages of specific positions also changes as people adapt, changing their position (1.2.1 Competitive Landscapes). **The more dynamic the landscape, the more we are forced from exploitation to exploration.** In other words, more static environments require more production while more dynamic environments require more strategy. The more dynamic our environment, the shorter the period of time a given position maintains its value. We are forced to move from old positions to new positions that are more valuable for exploitation. If there were not change in the landscape, there would be no new opportunities and everyone would be frozen in their existing positions (1.8.1 Creation and Destruction).

Illustration:

Let us make this very simple by considering a very small problem, finding the best place to eat.

1. Exploitation satisfies our immediate needs while exploration satisfies future needs. We can go to the best restaurant that we know or we can look for a better restaurant.

2. Exploration of the competitive landscape requires adapting thinking and strategy. Since there are a million restaurants, we need a method, that is, a strategy for finding the best ones. As we explore, we will discover new food preferences as well as new places so we will change our method as we learn more about our alternatives.

3. Exploitation of the competitive positions requires linear thinking and planning. If we are simply picking among the places we know, our job is much simpler: what are we in the mood for, what do we want to pay, what kind of time do we have.

4. We must strike a balance between exploration and exploitation. If we are always trying new restaurants, our average eating experience is going to be, by definition, average. If we are always going to the best restaurants that we know, our eating experiences cannot get better without those restaurants improving over time, a relatively rare occurrence.

5. *Positions are exploited and landscapes explored on both subjective and objective planes.* The shape of the landscape depends both upon our personal tastes and the tastes of others in our local area. People must have the objective skills to open and manage the restaurants to which we go. Those restaurants must be run well enough to survive and be supported by customers for them to survive.

6. *The relative advantages of positions for exploitation are constantly changing in the competitive landscape.* Our tastes change both from day to day and year to year. Restaurants are constantly opening and closing.

7. *The more dynamic the landscape, the more we are forced from exploitation to exploration..* In a very competitive market or in a volatile economy, our favorite restaurants are going to have a more difficult time surviving, so we are going to have to find new ones to replace them.

1.2.3 Position Complexity

Sun Tzu's seven key methods regarding how strategic positions arise from interactions in complex environments.

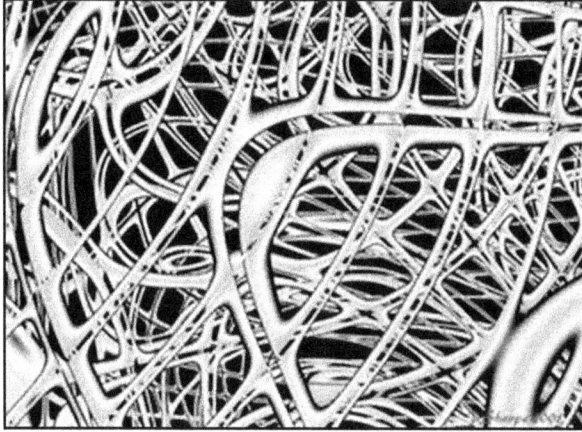

"War is very complicated and confusing. Battle is chaotic.
Nevertheless, you must not allow chaos."

Sun Tzu's The Art of War 5:4:1-3

"Out of intense complexities intense simplicities emerge."

Winston Churchill

General Principle: Positions emerge in unpredictable ways from their connections and interdependence on the positions of others.

Situation:

Positions exist as part of complex, adaptive systems that Sun Tzu called 'war' and we call 'competition.' His work explored the special nature of what we now call the "science of complexity." Today this science explains different aspects of biology, economics, ecology, sociology, physics and many other fields. The nature of complex systems inherently limits both our knowledge and control over positions. Complex systems do not work mechanically in a linear, predictable way. Complex systems are unpredictable because every part of them is adapting to change. Though competitive events are based on probabilities, we can never know the exact probabilities involved because behaviors are constantly adapting. Chaotic systems are unpredictable in deterministic ways because they follow fixed rules, but complex systems are both unpredictable and non-deterministic.

Opportunity: The good news is that a little understanding of complex systems can give us a big advantage. Most people are playing with mindsets that assume fixed rules, Sun Tzu saw that we have a tremendous opportunity to exploit their narrow expectations. While we cannot predict complex systems, they work by their own rules. These principles create new opportunities in unpredictable ways. We can leverage these ideas to our advantage. Our success starts by accepting the limits created by complexity (2.1.1 Information Limits, 3.1.6 Time Limitations). We advance our position by working within the constraints of complexity rather than trying to impose our own rules (3.2.1 Environmental Dominance).

Key Methods:

The following key methods describe the complexity of competitive positions.

1. Competitive landscapes are determined by the interactions of agents, each with its own agenda. These agents are us, both as individual people and the organizations we form. As agents, we each have our own agenda, consisting of our unique goals. We are free agents to the degree we can seek our own ends. The ways in which we interact determines our position (1.2.1 Competitive Landscapes).

2. Our positions are inherently connected to the positions of others and to our physical environment. These connections consist of the exchange of resources and information. These connections create a many-to-many network, where actions are communicated from many positions to many others (1.5.2. Group Methods).

3. *Our positions are interdependent on other positions and on our physical environments.* Our positions depend on the conditions and events in our physical environment. Our positions also depend on the positions of others and what they do. Our presence also affects the environment and what others do. Our dependencies are both physical and psychological, consisting of both fact and opinion. (1.2 Subobjective Positions).

4. *We all work to advance our positions based on our mental models*. These mental models determine how we perceive our position and choose our actions. These mental models have memory. They contain a history of previous positions. We use these models over and over again, our mental models can change over time as we learn. The complexity of our positions arises from our interactions with others who may use the same or very different mental models (2.2.2 Mental Models).

5. *Our actions generate reactions in the environment creating feedback loops.* Positive feedback reinforces actions. Negative feedback discourages actions. Positive feedback encourages actions, magnifying their effect and the dynamism of the environment, perhaps creating emergent properties. Negative feedback discourages actions, decreases their effects, stabilizes the environment, and channels efforts into alternative directions. Economic theory assumes diminishing returns, but in complex systems, feedback loops create more rewards and different forms of progress (1.8.2 The Adaptive Loop).

6. *As positions multiply, they become increasingly diverse, increasing the complexity of the landscape.* The uniqueness of each position generates a unique perspective. That unique perspective creates different mental models. Different mental models create different responses. Positions differentiate themselves. We develop specialized skills and organizations, increasing the diversity of the environment. This increasing diversity reshapes the competitive landscape (7.3 Strategic Innovation).

7. New positions emerge from competitive landscapes in unpredictable ways. In complex systems, the whole is greater than sum of its parts. Features emerge from interacting agents to create entirely new features and forms of value. This is known as "emergence." More is not just more in complex systems. It is often different. Progress takes the form of a phase transition from one state to another. Potential is unknown. New breakthroughs encourages further developments. In complexity, this is known as "path dependence." We depend upon new paths to create new opportunities. When competitive landscapes create novel features, we describe it as opening up new opportunities (3.2 Opportunity Creation).

8. The vast majority of changes in position will be small, but a few, rare big changes are possible. Complex systems are nonlinear. Small inputs can lead to major outcome swings. Results usually follow the power law distribution rather than a bell curve. The bigger the change, the more rare it will be. The more common the change, the smaller it will be (1.8.4 Probabilistic Process).

Illustration:

Let us illustrate these principles with a very simple illustration of a job position.

1. Competitive landscapes are determined by the interactions of agents, each with its own agenda. Our position at our workplace arises out of our interactions with other workers, customers, and everyone else we deal with in our job.

2. Our positions are connected to the positions of others and to our environment. We are connected to others by words and deeds. All jobs consist simply of exchanging information and materials with other people.

3. Our positions are interdependent on each other and on our environments. What we do affects what others do. What others do affects what we do. No man is an island if he has a job.

4. Our positions are advanced based on our mental models. We decide our actions directing our career based upon our mental models for managing our work life. These mental models affect how we see our native potential, our potential in the job market, and our potential at our current employer. We decide based upon those models whether to do what we are currently doing or seek a better position, either where we are or in another organization.

5. *All actions exist within feedback loops.* We hear about it when we make mistakes. We hear about it when we surprise people with a success. We hear about other opportunities in the job market.

6. *As positions multiply, they become increasingly diverse, increasing the complexity of the landscape.* Our work skills become more specialized as we deal with specific types of tasks. The more specialized our skill, the rarer it is and the more valuable it is.

7. *New positions emerge from competitive landscapes in unpredictable ways.* We cannot predict what opportunities will come our way.

8. *The vast majority of changes in position will be small, but a few, rare big changes are possible*. We will get many, many opportunities to improve our position in small ways. We will get very few opportunities to make a huge step up in responsibility.

1.3 Elemental Analysis

Sun Tzu's eight key methods defining the relevant components of all competitive positions.

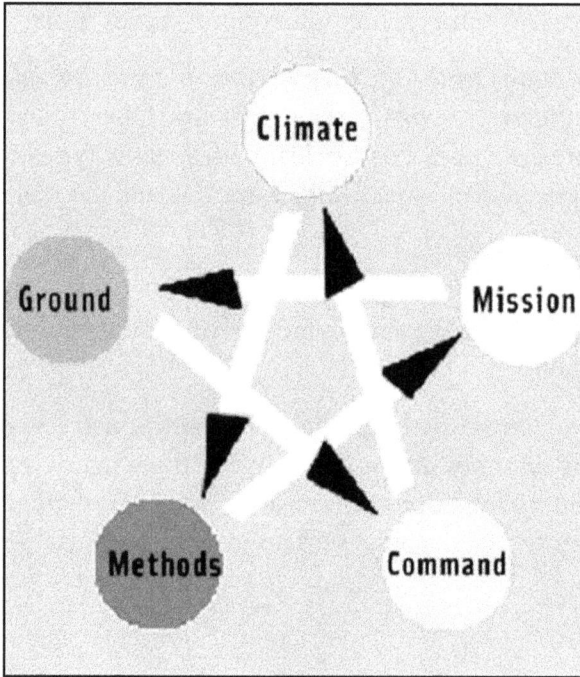

"Your skill comes from five factors. Study these factors when you plan war.
You must insist on knowing your situation."
Sun Tzu's The Art of War 1:1:6-8

"Space and time are not conditions in which we live; they are simply modes in which we think."
Albert Einstein

General Principle: Positions are compared according to mission, climate, ground, command, and methods.

Situation:

The strategic challenge is to find methods to make faster decisions in highly complex environments. In these complex, fast-changing environments, the human mind cannot deal with the vast amounts of detailed information. Literally thousands of factors can come into play in a given competitive situation. Multiple agents affect our positions. We don't even necessarily know those actors or their actions. We simply feel the affect of their decisions. Still, we must make decisions every day. We are never going to have time to collect and analyze all the data we want to make those decisions. Many bad decisions are simply unavoidable. The only way to find out that they are bad is to make them.

Opportunity:

Seeing strategic situations as relative positions is valuable because positions can be compared in an instant. We can learn what information is important and which is irrelevant. The comparison of a few relevant properties of positions can tell us their relative advantages. Choices on the basis of a few key elements of positions can be made quickly. When we identify the properties that make a position "better or worse," everything else falls into place. While there are literally hundreds of principles involved in making the best decisions about conditions, a few properties that all positions share lie at their core. Those few key strategic factors enable us to understand the relative strengths and weaknesses of any competing set of strategic positions.

Key Methods:

In physics, Einstein's **theory of relativity** requires the concept of space-time, a union of the dimensions of three dimensions of space and time. In using Art of War principles, strategic relatively similarly requires the union of five different dimensions:

*1. Mission is the dimension of the values determining strength and motivation*s. It is the organizing principle of a competitive force. Mission provides the core of a position's strength, connecting all the other elements. The values and goals of a mission determine its direction in the landscape. (1.6 Mission Values).

2. Climate is the dimension of change creating opportunities. It provides the temporary resources on which a position depends. It means all positions change over time. Without change, there can be no opportunities (1.4.1 Climate Shift).

3. Ground is the dimension of physical resources and persistent features. It is both where we compete and what we compete to control. The resources of ground provides rewards. Control of the ground gives a position stability ((1.4.2 Ground Features).

4. Command is the dimension of leadership and decision making. It is the realm of individual character. Decisions are not made by groups but by our individual choices. According to Sun Tzu, good warriors are distinguished by their ability to make productive decisions. The more productive our decisions, the more we extend our command (1.5.1 Command Leadership).

5. Methods are the dimension of group interactions for executing decisions. The most basic method is the division of labor. Methods define the realm of differentiated skills and our systems for putting them together to make the best use of resources. Methods are both competitive and productive (1.5.2. Group Methods).

6. All other principles for success relate directly to different aspects of these five key factors. Comparing strategic and competitive positions in the five dimensions of strategic space is the starting point for all meaningful strategic analysis. Most strategic analysis fails because it focuses on one or two of these areas, while ignoring the others (1.3.1 Competitive Comparison).

7. The five factors make it easier to envision a strategic situation in a tangible way. We can envision positions existing in a specific time and place. We can see them consisting of a group and a commander. We can understand the motivation that gives them purpose and direction. These elements allow us to understand the boundaries of positions, foresee their future directions, and predict the outcomes of meeting with surrounding positions (2.5 The Big Picture).

8. *These five characteristics can meaningfully map positions in any competitive arena.* Tools such as the Stratrix can help us map relative positions using these five dimensions. Just as Einstein's four dimensional space/time can be represented in a two-dimensional drawing to explain the operation of certain forces, the five dimensions of strategic space can be rendered in twodimensions, using the Institute's Stratrix tool (3.8 Strategic Matrix Analysis).

Illustration:

These five dimension affect every form of competition positioning: in business, relationships, sports, selling, military, and so on. Since every form of competition is a form of comparison, these factors always play into the conscious and subconscious ways positions are compared. As an illustration, let us contrast the areas of competition in business and personal relationships.

1. *Mission is the dimension of the values determining strength and motivation*s. Business mission is the goals and values the business shares with its customers, employees, and supporters. Relationship mission is what a given person is looking for in a relationship.

2. *Climate is the dimension of change creating opportunities*. Business climate is the forces of culture, technology, and economics driving business change in a market. Emotional climate is rise and fall of feelings over time that changes a relationship.

3. *Ground is the dimension of physical resources and persistent features*. Business ground is the marketplace of customers, suppliers, supporters, and competitors. The circle of intimacy is the personal connections that provide personal emotional resources.

4. *Command is the dimension of leadership and decision making*. Business command is the decision-making responsibilities of the organization. Character is attribute of personality that determine an individual's decision-making.

5. *Methods are the dimension of group interactions for executing decisions*. Business methods are the business processes, procedures, and other systems of producing value. Relationship interactions are the activities and habits of personal involvement on a daily basis.

6. *All other principles for success relate directly to different aspects of these five key factors*. The most successful businesses have relative strength in all five areas. The most successful relationships do as well.

7. *The five factors make it easier to envision a strategic situation in a tangible way*. Most businesses and most relationships focus on different aspects of their success formula, but usually miss the big picture of why it all works together around a core of mission.

8. *These five characteristics can meaningfully map positions in any competitive arena*. All such generic maps of businesses or relationships are over-simplifications, but they are useful. Their value is in simplifying complex positions.

1.3.1 Competitive Comparison

Sun Tzu's six key methods defining competition as the comparison of positions.

> "Creating a winning war is like balancing a coin of gold against a coin of silver.
> Creating a losing war is like balancing a coin of silver against a coin of gold."
>
> Sun Tzu's The Art of War 4:4:15-16

> "There is no comparison between that which is lost by not succeeding and that lost by not trying."
>
> Francis Bacon, Sr.

General Principle: Competition is based on the comparison of positions.

Situation:

People confuse competition with conflict because a lack of strategic skills leads inevitably to conflict. People think they hate competition because they prefer cooperation, but there can be no cooperation without competition. Most cooperation is inspired by our desire to be more successful in competition. We compete for the best partnerships, even the best spouses. In Sun Tzu's system, the opposite of cooperation is conflict not competition. Sun Tzu teaches "winning without conflict" as the most successful path in competition. Good strategy is impossible unless we understand what competition really is and why it is necessary.

Opportunity:

Science starts with clear definitions. In Sun Tzu's strategy, competition simply means making comparisons. Everyone makes comparisons all the time. Comparisons are necessary for decision making. Competition matters because our decisions matter. Since competition is comparison, information is critical to competition (2.1 Information Value). In the nineteenth century, the economist David Ricardo talked about competition as **comparative advantage**, which comes very close to Sun Tzu's ideas of relative positioning in competition. We all like being judges, but few us like being judged, but making comparisons and being compared are two sides of the same coin. The better we understand how competitive comparisons are made, the better we can understand where our opportunities lie (3.0 Identifying Opportunities).

Key Methods:

1. All competition is based on people making comparisons of characteristics. The elements of a position describe the most common points of comparison. Competition is the process by which people's positions are compared either in the judgments of others or by the physical outcome of events. Competing means seeking to advance our relative position in comparison to other positions. All strategic positions are judged by comparing them to other rival positions or alternative positions. This concept of comparison underlies *all* forms of competition. Unless a comparison is made, pitting one position against another, then no competition is possible (1.3 Elemental Analysis).

2. Comparisons are made among real alternatives. In competition, our position is measured either against the positions of others or our goals for our position. Positions are only measured relative to other positions, existing or desired. Though many forms of competition depend on the judgment of others, others do not. If we are alone on a desert island, we are competing against nature on the objective basis of an outcome, our survival (1.1 Position Paths).

3. Comparisons are based on past outcomes and judgments about future outcomes. The comparison among different positions is determined either by a physical outcome, by other people's judgment, or by a combination of the two. These comparisons are the basis of the objective and subjective natures of positions (1.2 Subobjective Positions).

4. Different areas of comparisons have different rules and standards for comparison. Every area of skill, every contest, and every other type of competition has rules by which its comparisons are made. When comparisons are made by outcomes, the rules govern what actions are allowed. When comparisons are made by opinions, the rules provide standards and guidelines for those judgments (1.2.1 Competitive Landscapes).

5. All rewards are attained from successful comparisons. For a comparison to be interesting, the comparison must be tied to a reward or payoff of some type. Competition is not just about winning any comparison, but winning those comparisons that pay according to our values (1.6 Mission Values).

6. *Both cooperation and conflict are based on comparison. Cooperating means working to a common goal.* We can join together with others to advance our position because by joining with others we can improve our relative position in many types of groups. Conflict means working for opposing goals. Direct competition means having incompatible goals, such as two competitors seeking the same, exclusive position. In evaluating relationships, we look for relationships that will support our goals and try to avoid conflicts that take us further from our goals (1.6.1 Shared Mission).

Illustration:

Let us look at how these key methods of comparison work for a wide variety of very different forms of competition.

1. All competition is based on people making comparisons of characteristics. A sporting event is a comparison of the capabilities of two opposing teams. A buying decision is a comparison of alternative uses of money. A job interview is a comparison of job candidates.

2. Comparisons are made among real alternatives. In sporting season, the position of one team is based on a comparison with the positions of the other teams in its group. In an evaluation of job performance, however, our position might be compared against our performance expectations, in the context of other employees' performances.

3. Comparisons are based on past outcomes and judgments about future outcomes. In sports, positions are based on outcomes of games. In a beauty contest, positions are determined by the opinions of judges. In a hiring decision, our position might be partly based on past outcomes and partly based on judgments of future potential.

4. Different areas of comparisons have different rules and standards for comparison. In sports, players must know the rules and what plays are allowed and which are penalized. In a dog show, judges must know the standards by which each breed is measured.

5. All rewards are attained from successful comparisons. In war, winning a costly battle can lead to losing the entire war. In a relationship, winning an argument can cost us a friendship.

6. Both cooperation and conflict are based on comparison. In sports, success is based upon the cooperation within the team. Military battles do not occur unless both armies think that they can win.

1.3.2 Element Scalability

Sun Tzu's seven key methods regarding how positions are analyzed by both component positions and elements.

"You control a large group the same as you control a few.
You just divide their ranks correctly."
Sun Tzu's The Art of War 5:1:1

"Two things are as big as the man who possesses them -
neither bigger nor smaller. One is a minute, the other a
dollar."
Channing Pollock

General Principle: Positions and their elements are scalable and self-referencing.

Situation:

We can get confused about strategic positions because they exist on a variety of different scales. Positions exist within larger positions. We can see positions close up or from a distance. A given nation's economy has a position within the world economy. An industry has a position within a nation's economy. A business has a position within an industry. An employee has a position within a business. The five elements defining the basic characteristics of a position also scale, reflecting each other at different levels. If we look at one of the key elements, for example, Mission, we can analyze it by breaking it down into the five elements.

Opportunity:

The mental models of Sun Tzu's strategy simplify complexity (2.2.2 Mental Models). We summarize volumes of confusing detail in a simpler picture. Looking more closely at a given element of a position helps us find the key element within the key element that we can best leverage as an opportunity (3.1.4 Openings). To do this analysis correctly, we must understand the principles about how positions and their elements scale. While there is always value in seeing the bigger picture, drilling down into the details can be useful only when we are trying to address very specific strategic issues (2.5 The Big Picture). Strategic positions contain a limitless amount of detail, but we only have time to access a very limited amount of it (2.1.1 Information Limits).

Key Methods:

The following seven key methods describe the different scales of positions.

1. Group positions can be broken down into the positions of its component groups and finally its individuals. We use these different scales in order to develop a more complete perspective.

2. Container positions provide the context for the relative comparisons of their component positions. Larger groups have positions that contain smaller positions of the smaller groups and individuals of which they are made. As individuals, we have smaller positions within the larger groups to which we belong (2.0 Developing Perspective).

3. An individual's position can be broken down into overlapping positions in different competitive arenas. As individuals, we have positions in a variety of family, career, business, and social circles. Looking at these overlapping positions gives us perspective on the balances that people strike in their lives (1.2.1 Competitive Landscapes).

4. Every element of a position can itself be broken down into the five key elements. Breaking down elements into more detailed sub-elements allows us to see more deeply into parts of positions and situations. Each element has unique characteristics that can be better understood in terms of the other four elements and self-reflexively, in terms of itself. We use the five key elements as different viewing angles to give us more perspective. Looking at elements within elements gives us depth of perspective (1.3 Elemental Analysis).

5. The elements from larger positions are greater than the sum of the elements of smaller positions. Elements within positions can add to the elements of larger positions, but new elemental characteristics can emerge from the group as a whole. Since some of the elements of component positions can cancel each other out, the resulting elements within a given group position can be very different than the elements of all the individual positions within it (1.2.3 Position Complexity).

6. The direction of a larger position is the sum of directions of its component positions. In other words, the element of mission must be shared to create direction in a larger position. The other four elements can reside in different parts of a position, but mission must tie the larger position together. The group falls apart or flies apart or stays where it is if mission is not shared (1.6.1 Shared Mission).

7. The direction of component positions is affected but not determined by the direction of larger positions. If a container position is improving or declining, all of its component positions will tend to improve or decline as well. This is very similar to the way the direction of the climate affects a position but doesn't determine it (1.4.1 Climate Shift).

Illustration:

These abstract key methods are easier to understand if we provide some examples.

1. Group positions can be broken down into the positions of its component groups and finally its individuals. An industry is made of component businesses. Those businesses are made of different product divisions. In the end, it all comes down to individual people.

2. *Container positions provide the context for the relative comparisons of their component positions.* The business position of an individual is best understood within their role in their business and their business's role in their industry,

3. An individual's position can be broken down into overlapping positions in different competitive arenas. A person can be very successful in their career and this fact can either help or hurt his or her family position. Since time resources are always limited, career competes with family, but since success in business produces other resources, such as money, it can help family position.

4. Every element of a position can itself be broken down into the five key elements. For example, we break the element of leadership into 1) caring about mission, 2) courage in facing climate changes, 3) intelligence to know the ground, 4) discipline in using methods, and 5) trustworthiness relating to leadership. Knowing that leader is weak in a given area, for example courage, we can better predict his or her behavior.

5. The elements from larger positions are greater than the sum of the elements of smaller positions. The mission of a company is not the sum of all of its employees' missions. It is the intersection of its employees' missions.

6. *The direction of a larger position is the sum of directions of its component positions.* If the majority of companies within a given industry are improving their position, the industry is improving its position as well.

7. *The direction of component positions is affected but not determined by the direction of larger positions*. A company's position can be declining along with its entire industry, but improving relative to its competition. Both of these factors are important in understanding the company's real position. If the position company is declining, the position of most but not all of its employees will be declining as well.

1.4.0 The External Environment

Sun Tzu's seven key methods defining the key external conditions shaping strategic positions.

"You must know the battleground.
You must know the time of battle."
Sun Tzu's The Art of War 6:6:1-2

"Man must cease attributing his problems to his environment, and learn again to exercise his will - his personal responsibility in the realm of faith and morals."
Albert Schweitzer

General Principle: The key external conditions are the temporary and persistent features and resources.

Situation:

External conditions are all properties of our positions that we cannot directly control. We have three problems in dealing with these environmental conditions. First, there are a vast number of such conditions in a competitive environment. So many that all external conditions cannot be known. Our second problem is knowing which of these conditions are important to our position and which are not. Most of us fail to recognize the environmental forces that affect us. We are distracted by events that are recent and noisy while ignoring other conditions that are much more important. Finally, our last problem is knowing how to relate all these conditions to create a comprehensive picture of our situation.

Opportunity:

Given a clear mental model for understanding which conditions are strategically important and which are not, we can quickly filter out the most relevant information from the vast amount of data in the competitive environment (2.2.2 Mental Models). We can quickly see what key pieces we are missing. From a powerful model, we can develop a complete picture, not only of our competitive position in the context of the larger environment, but just as importantly the position of others and how their position relates and compares to our own. This mental model also gives us a framework for organizing a flood of information from our environment so that it facilitates making the right choices automatically. This organized picture allows us to see where our opportunities lie.

Key Methods:

The seven most general key methods for recognizing and categorizing these external conditions are:

1. We must first recognize the dynamic elements of the environment. Sun Tzu calls these temporary elements the conditions of climate. These are the formless resources, attitudes, and events that are constantly shifting and changing situations. The most important of such resources is our time. (1.4.1 Climate Shift).

2. We must then recognize the persistent elements of the environment. Sun Tzu calls these stable elements the conditions of the ground. These are the material resources, characteristics, and forms of our environment. These are the features that make a position valuable over time (1.4.2 Ground Features).

3. To better understand the changing climate, separate conscious choices from natural phenomena. Conscious choices arise from the strategic positions of others and can be analyzed by strategic methods. Natural phenomena are understood through other forms of science. Some climate events are a combination of both, the natural but unintended consequences of our choices. Natural phenomena are more predictable than human interaction. Such interactions create deep complexity of non-deterministic unpredictability (1.2.3 Position Complexity).

4. To categorize persistent fixtures of the environment, we separate actors from objects. Objects are more controllable than actors. Again, actors are amenable to strategic methods while objects are amenable to production methods. Groups of actors form a single actor when they work together. With the proper methods, we can shape objects in a highly predictable way, but in working with people, our results are always a matter of probabilities (1.8.4 Probabilistic Process).

5. We can rank all environmental conditions by their relative size. Conditions have size both in the physical sense and in the psychological sense. Psychological size depends on connections, the number of people affected by a condition and the degree to which they are affected. Events and temporary resources are measured in duration in time and the breadth of their impact. Stable features and resources can be counted and measured because they are tangible. These comparisons are the basis of all knowledge (2.6 Knowledge Leverage).

6. We can rank all environmental conditions by their proximity to our current position. Strategic proximity is measured in both physical distance and the amount of learning required. Proximity defines our immediate environment, that is, the conditions that have the largest and most immediate effect upon us. Events have proximity both in time and space while fixtures have proximity only in space. The concept of strategic distance is critical in understanding the impact of environmental conditions (4.4 Strategic Distance).

7. Impact of external conditions is measured in their size times their proximity. The amount of impact from events and actors is a combination of their proximity and size. Both their number of connections and the proximity of those connections are important in terms of impact (2.3.1 Action and Reaction).

Illustration:

The seven most general key methods for recognizing and categorizing these external conditions are:

1. *We must first recognize the dynamic elements of the environment.* Sunrise is a dynamic element. A purchase is an event. Our thoughts, actions, and emotions are all changing and shifting.

2. *We must then recognize the persistent elements of the environment.* The sun is a fixture of the environment. A buyer is a fixture of the economy. Our bodies, houses, and cars are persistent.

3. *To better understand the changing climate, separate conscious choices from natural phenomena*. A purchase is a choice. Sunrise is a natural phenomena. A traffic jam is a combination of both, the result of many conscious choices interfering with each other creating an unintended event.

4. *To categorize persistent fixtures of the environment, we separate actors from objects*. A buyer is an actor. The sun is an object. A company is an actor, but a city (separate from its government and buildings) is more like an object.

5. *We can rank all environmental conditions by their relative size*. A big company of many people is a bigger actor than a small company of fewer people. In strategic terms, a hurricane that hits the coast is psychologically bigger than one that stays out at sea because it affects more people.

6. *We can rank all environmental conditions by their proximity to our current position.* A hurricane that hits a coast near us is more important than one that hits somewhere else. A company in our industry affects us more than those in unrelated industries.

7. ***Impact of external conditions is measured in their size times their proximity.*** A slowdown in an industry has a narrower impact than a general recession. A recession in America has more impact on Americans than one in Europe.

1.4.1 Climate Shift

Sun Tzu's nine key key methods regarding forces of environmental change shaping temporary conditions.

*"You control your army by controlling its morale.
As a general, you must be able to control emotions."*
Sun Tzu's The Art of War 7:5:1-2

*"Temperament lies behind mood; behind will, lies the
fate of character. Then behind both, the influence of
family the tyranny of culture; and finally the power of
climate and environment; and we are free, only to the
extent we rise above these."*
John Burroughs

General Principle: Climate describes temporary external conditions, events, and the forces driving them.

Situation:

The passage of time plays a huge part in Sun Tzu's strategy. We experience the world as a series of events. Events affecting our strategic position come at us from many different directions. The problem is seeing these events in useful context rather than as a random series of happenings. Today's media makes this problem worse since it makes its living by bringing us more and more events. Our challenge is putting all those events into a coherent strategic picture. The world of events is the world of change. Most of us fear change because we fear the unknown. The more change we experience, the more chaotic conditions appear to be. The change seems without direction or meaning.

Opportunity:

Sun Tzu puts change into the context of the weather and climate. In the climate, changing events are both the cause and effect of all the energy in our environment. The energy of change creates opportunities. Without change, new opportunities to advance our position would not arise. All positions would be static. In societies that suppress change, people live and die in more or less the same state and, for most of them, that state is abject poverty.

The more dynamic external conditions, the more opportunities we have. The richest nations throughout history have been the fastest changing, that is, those at the center of events. The fact that most people fear change creates even more opportunities for those who are willing to embrace it.

Key Methods:

We use the concept of climate to help us discuss and evaluate the nature, direction, and the forces driving change.

1. Climate describes all external conditions that shift, evolve, and reverse themselves over time. In the simplest terms, *climate* describes what changes in our environment in contrast to the ground, which describes what is relatively stable. Of course, everything changes, especially our position, which changes even if we do nothing (1.1.1 Position Dynamics).

2. The primary resource of climate is time. We can only make decisions in the now, but those decisions factor in what has come before and what we expect in the future. Unlike all other resources, we each get the exact same amount of time every day. The only difference is what we do with it. Some of us kill time. Others of us are killed by time. The passage of time and its affect upon positions is all part of the cycle of the seasons in Sun Tzu's system (1.8.3 Cycle Time).

3. *Physical changes in climate affect our capacities*. The physical manifestation of time is movement. As time passes, movement changes the relationships of our physical proximity. This physical change affects our capability for various activities and our access to physical resources. Like the movement of pieces on a chessboard, the movement of people and objects over time affects what activities are possible. This is the objective side of climate (1.2 Subobjective Positions).

4. *Intellectual changes in climate affect our attitudes which determines our activities*. To categorize events, we separate conscious choices from natural phenomena. The choices in competition cannot be separated from emotion. Emotion is the trigger for action. The stronger the emotion, the more likely action is. The ability to get people to act is determined by the emotional climate. This is the subjective side of climate (8.5 Leveraging Emotions).

5. *Except for the increase of methods knowledge, all trends reverse automatically when they reach an extreme*. No trend keeps going up or down forever. Only learning and knowledge accumulate predictably over time. Many trends reverse themselves in predictable cycles that we can often recognize based on history. In straight-line trends, we do not usually recognize the potential for change, thinking that it will continue forever (3.2.5 Dynamic Reversal).

6. *The most valuable trends for decision making are cyclic*. They occur at regular intervals. These cyclic trends are driven by the balancing forces of complementary opposites. All such cycles eventually reverse themselves automatically because the underlying forces driving them balance each other. According to Sun Tzu's analysis, without these underlying balancing forces, all nature would dissolve into chaos. Only some cycles repeat themselves at regular intervals. Trends that depend on physical phenomena are more predictable than those that depend on choices. Physical trends are more predictable than emotional. (3.2.3 Complementary Opposites).

7. All positions age and are eventually destroyed as new positions are created. This is the cycle of birth and death. Everything that grows stronger eventually grows old and dies, including strategic positions (1.8.1 Creation and Destruction).

8. Every competitive arena is associated with its own climate. In the competitive environment, climate cannot be separated from ground anymore than time can be separated from space. However, we can talk about different characteristics and aspects of climate as distinct from ground, just as we can discuss aspects of the dimension of time as distinct from the dimensions of space (1.4 The External Environment).

9. Good timing depends upon understanding the trends of climate. Timing is knowing when to move and when to stay put. Many strategic moves are time sensitive. Situations are fluid. When a situation clearly demands a specific response, we must do so instantly, before the situation changes. It is also the knowledge of how to create and use strategic momentum. (7.4 Timing).

Illustration:

Each of these concepts is briefly illustrated below. We use the concept of climate to help us discuss and evaluate the nature, direction, and the forces driving change.

1. Climate describes all external conditions that shift, evolve, and reverse themselves over time. Business has a climate that is constantly changing. Relationships also have a climate. There is a job climate, industry climate, national climates and so on. All types of climate are both the result of change and the cause of it, affecting people's decisions.

2. The primary resource of climate is time. The business climate today is different from yesterday's and tomorrow's, but in each of these days, we all have only 24 hours to make our decisions.

3. *Physical changes in climate affect our capacities*. When it is rainy and muddy outside, we cannot travel as far, quickly, or easily. When it is light, we can see where we are going. When it is too cold or too hot, we tire more quickly.

4. *Intellectual changes in climate affect our attitudes which determines our activities*. If people are depressed, confused, or uncertain, it is difficult to get them to act, say in a depressed economy. If people are either very afraid or very confident, action is easy.

5. *Except for the increase of methods knowledge, all trends reverse automatically when they reach an extreme*. Day is followed by night, summer by winter. Happiness is balanced by sadness, courage by fear. A market that goes up will eventually come down, except to the extent it is driven by the growth of human knowledge.

6. *The most valuable trends for decision making are cyclic.* The timing of day and night are predictable but the rise and fall of markets is less so. However, the fact that markets rise and fall is critical in making good investment decisions.

7. *All positions age and are eventually destroyed as new positions are created*. People grow stronger and more capable as they mature from children to adults. As they get older, they begin to physically and psychologically decline. The same cycle applies to businesses, nations, and technologies.

8. *Every competitive arena is associated with its own climate*. The climate in California is different than the climate in Maine. The climate of the transportation industry is different from the climate in manufacturing. The climate of baseball is different from the climate of soccer.

9. *Good timing depends upon understanding the trends of climate.* The timing of day and night are predictable but the rise and fall of markets are not. The best time to start a business is during a recession. If we can survive financially during hard times, when the eventual reversal takes place, economic growth will grow the business. The worst time to start a business is during boom times when bad practices are forgiven by a favorable environment. Companies than can only survive during good times are weeded out during bad.

1.4.2 Ground Features

Sun Tzu's ten key methods defining the persistent resources that we can control.

"Some commanders are not skilled in making adjustments to find an advantage. They can know the shape of the terrain.
Still, they cannot exploit the opportunities of their ground."

Sun Tzu's The Art of War 7:1:16

"Innovation is the specific instrument of entrepreneurship. The act that endows resources with a new capacity to create wealth."

Peter F. Drucker

General Principle: Ground describes external conditions that persist over time and provide resources.

Situation:

Where we are now doesn't dictate where we can go in the long-term, but it does dictate where we can go next. We are confined by our position's location. We move according to the laws governing space. The challenge is understanding the laws that govern strategic space. Every location has its own shape and form. Every place is connected through space to nearby places. Place is inherently much more complicated than time. Understanding the complex nature of location and its many characteristics and capacities is at the heart of Sun Tzu's strategy. Without the resources that we get from our physical position, we could not continue to survive, much less compete. In a modern world, we make a mistake in taking these resources, such as food and water, for granted, not recognizing the work that has been required throughout history to attain them.

Opportunity:

The benefit of every location is the resources that it offers. Every physical location offers resources. The most basic resource that every position offers is its proximity to other positions. Proximity decreases our costs in moving to better position with more resources. We win that ability to use the resources of a given place through competition, but we translated that control into resources through production (1.9 Competition and Production). Strategic methods allow us to expand our control over our space. The more successfully we compete, the more area we control. We advance our position both by expanding our area of control and by moving to new, more bountiful areas.

Key Methods:

We use the concept of ground to help us discuss and evaluate the nature, shape, and properties of a given location when compared to other locations.

1. Ground is the term we use to discuss space, place, and location. Ground describes all external conditions that persist over time. In the complementary opposite *climate,* which describes what changes over time. The ***ground*** describes what persists despite the changes of time (<u>1.4.1 Climate Shift</u>).

 2. *Ground is the store of all persistent resources*. The ground is a source of resources that persist over time. These resources are both physical and psychological. These resources are the rewards we get from controlling the ground (<u>8.0 Winning Rewards</u>).

 3. *We access the resources of ground through our control over it*. To gain resources from the ground, we must first win control over it. This control allows us to use the ground productively. We win control of the ground through competition and get rewards from it through production (<u>1.9 Competition and Production</u>).

 4. *We earn control over ground through competition.* The ground is both where we compete and what we compete for. For gladiators, the ground was the games in the coliseum because their performance in them was the source of all their rewards. In business, we define the ground in terms of marketplaces and their customers. In sports, the ground is the market for customers, the market for sports talent, and the actual playing field, depending upon your focus (<u>1.3.1 Competitive Comparison</u>).

 5. *The physical nature of ground determines the physical resources it provides*. The physical characteristics of the ground affects how we can use it and what forms of resources it offers. Those characteristics start with physical space itself and its proximity to other locations. In terms of defending and advancing positions, the conditions of the ground is evaluated in terms of distances, obstacles, and dangers. We categorize different forms of the ground in terms uneven, fast-changing, and uncertain. Other conditions define the six extreme forms of ground. Still others discuss the terrain in terms of how it affects our relationships with others. This is the objective side of ground (<u>1.2 Subobjective Positions</u>).

 6. *The intellectual nature of ground provides psychological resources*. In order to make decisions, people compare the characteristics of both objects and actors, positioning them in their minds. While emotional attitudes create climate, people's skills, knowledge, and opinions persist over time making them part of the ground, the mental terrain. This is the subjective side of ground (1.3.1 Competitive Comparison).

7. Most of the objective and subjective aspects of ground can be discussed in the same terms. The conditions of our mental terrain can be categorized using many of the same shape and form characteristics that we use to talk about physical space. We can only make good decisions about conditions when we have learned how to recognize them in physical terms (2.2.3 Standard Terminology).

8. The resources available in any one position are limited. A part is less than the whole. Some ground has fewer resources than all ground. Only a certain amount of resources can be produced over a given period of time from a given location. This limitation is partially driven by our limited knowledge. (3.1.1 Resource Limitations).

9. Our control over the ground is also limited. We never have complete control over the ground because our knowledge of nature is limited and because we compete with others (8.1.2 Control Limits).

10. We can only learn the value of controlling the ground after winning control. This problem creates one of the fundamental challenges of strategy because it means that we cannot predict the value of ground until we control it (2.3.2 Reaction Unpredictability).

Illustration:

Each of these concepts is briefly illustrated below.

We use the concept of ground to help us discuss and evaluate the nature, shape, and properties of a given location when compared to other locations.

1. Ground is the term we use to discuss space, place, and location. In terms of the physical space, locations in California are different than locations in Maine. In business space, the competitive arena in the transportation industry is different from the ground in manufacturing. As a playing field, the ground in baseball in different from the ground in soccer or American football.

2. Ground is the store of all persistent resources. The capabilities of our bodies are the minimum physical resources of the ground. Gold mines and oil wells produce other types of ground resources. Our reputations and knowledge are other forms of ground resources.

3. We access the resources of ground through our control over it. The only ground that we are born controlling is our own bodies. Our property, position at work, and position in the community are all forms of ground that we earn over time.

4. We earn control over ground through competition. If we were gladiators, the ground would be the coliseum because our performance there is the source of all potential awards. In business, we define the ground in terms of marketplaces and their customers. In sports, the ground is the market for customers, the market for sports talent, and the actual playing field, depending upon your focus.

5. The physical nature of ground determines the physical resources it provides. Food, water, metal, oil, and the invaluable resource of proximity come from the element ground.

6. The intellectual nature of ground provides psychological resources. People who have always bought a certain brand of car or voted for a particular party or to prefer doing a certain type of work all have a certain mental terrain.

7. Most of the objective and subjective aspects of ground can be discussed in the same terms. "High ground" is both a physical and a psychological strategic concept. Visibility, barriers, area, and almost every other aspect of the physical ground have their psychological parallels.

8. The resources available in any one position are limited. The abilities of a group of people are more than the abilities of any one person or subgroup of that group.

9. Our control over the ground is also limited. We control our bodies, but we cannot control our liver function. All jobs have limits on their authority. Even our control over our own property is controlled by a host of laws and conventions.

10. *We can only learn the value of controlling the ground after winning control*. We don't know how profitable a business is until we start it. We don't know the burdens of a management position until we win it.

1.5.0 Competing Agents

Sun Tzu's seven key methods regarding characteristics of competitors.

"Which method of command works? Which group of forces has the strength?"

Sun Tzu's The Art of War 1:2:7

"When once a decision is reached and execution is the order of the day, dismiss absolutely all responsibility and care about the outcome."

William James

General Principle: Competitors must make and execute decisions affecting their position.

Situation:

As competitors, that is, as agents or actors in a competitive landscape, we must make decisions and execute actions to improve our strategic position. Choices must be made, but those choices must be executed as well. Decisions and execution are two sides of the same coin. The problem is that most people do not have a clear mental model of what competitors are and how they interact. Competing agents consist of specific components. These characteristics play important roles in how a given competitor makes decisions and executes them. Without a model for understanding competitors, we skip from one competitive characteristic to the next, trying to figure out what role it plays. We miss certain important elements while fixating on a few. Only through luck and chance do we hit upon what is and is not important in a given situation with a given set of competing agents.

Opportunity: When we have a clear model of the key elements of a competitor, we can compare our abilities to the abilities of others. This comparison is the basis of competitive positions (1.3.1 Competitive Comparison). When we have a clear model about how competing agents interact, we can predict behavior much more easily. Sun Tzu provides a framework for understanding competing agents that we can refine over time. The skills that Sun Tzu teaches help competing agents make better decisions and better execute those decisions. Making decisions that we can execute and executing the decisions that we make are two sides of the same coin in Sun Tzu's system.

Key Methods:

The following seven key methods describe the key aspect of competing agents, ourselves, our rivals, and our supporters.

1. The competitive landscape is made up of competing agents who are compared. Competition is comparison. As agents, we act to improve our relative positions. As agents, we are compared by judgments. Those judgments are based both on opinions and outcomes. In many landscapes, we act as both agents and judges. In other landscapes, judgments are made apart from the agents themselves. Agents can be individuals or organizations made of individuals (1.2.1 Competitive Landscapes).

2. *Agents' decisions are motivated by their missions.* As agents, we all act with purpose. Our purpose is to satisfy our needs, values, and desires. All of us are motivated by our own personal mission. Individuals join into organizations to satisfy their mutual goals (1.6 Mission Values).

3. *Making competitive decisions requires the clear authority of command.* If the competing agent is one individual, that person is responsible for making his or her own decisions. If the agent is a group of people, the command role of making decisions can be divided into various areas of responsibility. Success of the organization demands clear lines of authority. People must know who has command in a given area. One individual must clearly have the final responsibility (1.5.1 Command Leadership).

4. *Methods for execution require methods combining personal skills and group systems*. Skills are the capability of an individual. Systems are the interaction of individuals within a group. Without skills and systems, decisions cannot be executed (1.5.2. Group Methods).

5. *Command and methods require each other.* Actions cannot be executed without a decision, but leaders cannot make decisions without taking into account how decisions are executed. Our ability to execute certain activities directs our decision making. Our decisions direct what actions we attempt to execute. These two components are complementary opposites, representing two different aspects of the same unified process (3.2.3 Complementary Opposites).

6. *Command and methods are always limited, specialized to fit in their position.* No person can do everything. No organization, no matter how large, can masters all skills and systems. A given set of decision-making and execution skills are developed to fit a given position (8.1.2 Control Limits).

7. *The model of command and methods is scalable.* It applies to an individual making and executing decisions about his or her position. It also applies the the largest organizations and how those organizations make decisions regarding their positions. At each level, the leader of a division picks the leaders under him or her.

Organization describes who has the authority for making specific types of decisions and who has the responsibility for executing those decisions (1.3.2 Element Scalability).

Illustration:

These ideas are fairly simple, but we offer some examples below.

1. The competitive landscape is made up of competing agents who are compared. In commercial society, we are both agents and judges. We compete either individually or as part of organizations for the dollars of customers. As customers, we judge other agents who compete for our dollars but we also compete for products in situations such as auctions. In sports, teams compete as agents, but the judgments are made by referees according to the rules of the game. In politics, politicians are agents who compete for the judgment of voters.

2. Agents' decisions are motivated by their missions. We work at our jobs to get an income. The more income we have the more desires we can satisfy. In romantic relationships, we compete for attention and commitment depending on the type of attention and commitment we desire. In sports, we compete to win games, but the individual athletes are also competing for recognition and attention.

3. Making competitive decisions requires the clear authority of command. Organizations flounder when they do not have a clear leader making clear decisions. I often see this problem when my family gets together. Since no one of us is in charge, we have a terrible time making decisions about what to do and who should do it. In the end, events only take shape once areas of responsibility are carved out.

4. Methods for execution require methods combining personal skills and group systems. In order to open a restaurant, we need to have access to a range of skills: cooking, menu-making, purchasing ingredients, selecting a location, negotiating a lease, and so on. While we can learn skills by doing, trial and error is an expensive form of education.

5. *Command and methods require each other.* It doesn't make any sense to decide to make cake if no one knows a recipe for making it. It doesn't make sense to bake a cake just because we know how if no one wants to eat cake.

6. *Command and methods are always limited, specialized to fit in their position.* Companies that have tried to master a wide variety of skills have consistently failed. The whole concept of "outsourcing" arises from the recognition of limits.

7. *The model of command and methods is scalable.* Large organizations run by distributing leadership and execution responsibilities to various groups. Within Wal-Mart, there are purchasing and selling divisions. In the selling divisions, there are geographic managers responsible for managing groups of stores. Each store has a manager. Each department within a store has a manager. At each time of day, someone is at least temporarily responsible for every area.

1.5.1 Command Leadership

Twelve key methods regarding individual decision-making (leaders).

"Next is the commander.
He must be smart, trustworthy, caring, brave, and
strict."

Sun Tzu's The Art of War 1:1:2829

"When once a decision is reached and execution is the
order of the day, dismiss absolutely all responsibility and
care about the outcome."

William James

General Principle: Leaders must make command decisions based on their training and character.

Situation:

In controlled environments, we are working with objects, and our success depends on knowing the right set of procedures to follow. Competitive environments are different. When we are on the front lines of competition, our success depends on the decisions that we make. Our decisions must take into account the changing conditions of our environment. Decisions must be made quickly, often with a minimum of information. Many of these decisions are automatic responses to conditions. The first problem that we must address is the one of taking personal responsibility. The second challenge is developing the personality characteristics that result in good decisions.

Opportunity:

Trained front-line leaders can recognize the key characteristics of a situation and respond instantly. They know which responses are the most likely to be successful. When we have a clear understanding of leadership, we can pick better leaders. When we understand the key characteristics of leaders, we can measure both ourselves and others against those standards. We can know who we can trust. We can predict who will make good decisions and what mistakes others are likely to make. When we understand how leadership really works, we can make the correct decisions more quickly without having to worry about making serious mistakes. The mistakes we do make are those from which we can learn.

Key Methods:

The following key methods apply to the element of leadership command:

1. Command is the responsibility of the individual. Leaders must make their decisions alone, and individuals must assume command within their own lives. There is no such thing as a group decision. Groups can only concur with a decision made by an individual. The individuals within a group each make their own decisions about whether to agree or battle with a suggested decision (1.5 Competing Agents).

2. We are in command when we are making decisions for our own goals. Even when we are following the command decisions of others, we usually find ourselves making decisions for ourselves through the course of the day. Even when following an organization's rules about how those decisions are to be made, we are using our own judgment in each moment (1.6 Mission Values).

3. The more successful we are at making decisions, the more people turn to us as a leader. The decisions of command with many followers may have a broader impact than the decisions of an individual, but every individual has to take command responsibility if only for the course of their own lives. The skills of decision-making are the same for a leader of millions and for each of us *leading* our own lives (1.9.2 Span of Control).

4. As leaders, we must make decisions whether we want to or not. When we are in command, we are making a decision even when we choose to avoid or delay a decision. The decision not to decide is also a decision. The decision to continue doing what we have been doing is a decision as well (1.8.1 Creation and Destruction).

5. Command makes decisions to respond to events. While we tend to think of "events" as the actions of others, more broadly "events" simply represent the discovery of new information about conditions in our environment. Our senses are constantly picking up information from the environment, but not all of it is new. It is the new information that triggers the leader's decision-making machinery. Some new information is generated by change. This is information from the climate. However, other information has been there all the time, but it is new to us because we discover it for the first time. This is information from the ground, specifically information from learning more about the ground (5.1.1 Event Pressure).

6. Leaders must know which strategic areas require foresight and analysis. The most basic command activities require working at building up a strategic picture of the situation. While many command decisions require snap, gut decisions, those decisions are based on a carefully cultivated strategic picture. Other decisions, such as the use of surprises, require preparation beforehand (3.0 Identifying Opportunities).

7. Leaders must train their minds for snap decision-making.
Our senses are exposed to a flood of information during the events
of the day, and we are not necessarily consciously aware of it all.
Our brains work on the pre-conscious level filtering that information to select the ideas that are important enough to penetrate our
awareness. Our brains are continually making low-level decisions
about what information is important enough to bring to the attention of the higher-level decision-making processes of our conscious
minds (5.3 Reaction Time).

**8. Small command decisions have the biggest impact on our
lives over time.** Success is less about individual decisions as it is
about the general course of our decisions and the quality of the decision that we are making over time. No matter how well we analyze
and train, we are going to make plenty of mistakes. The key is to
learn from them. If we do, many individual decisions, even those
that seem very insignificant at the time, can have a huge impact on
the course of our lives over large spans of time. To stay in command, we must decide what is the best use of our time at every
moment of every day (1.8.2 The Adaptive Loop).

9. Leadership requires five qualities of character. Since leaders
are continuously making both subconscious and conscious decisions
in an instant, command is a product of our character. The five qualities of leadership character are tied closely to the five key factors
that define a strategic position (1.3 Elemental Analysis).

- *Caring* means devotion to the shared mission or goals.
- *Courage* means confronting the uncontrollable conditions of a changing climate.
- *Knowledge* means understanding the rules of winning
  resources from the conditions of the ground.
- *Trustworthiness* means honoring commitments to others
  in the realm of methods.
- *Discipline* means executing the decisions required of
  leadership.

**10. A lack of character qualities in a leader, show up in five
different ways.** A leader who lacks these skills is unable to improve
his or her position (3.5 Strength and Weakness):

- A lack of caring loses sight of the mission in dealing with events.
- A lack of courage cannot discover opportunities in adversity.
- A lack of knowledge fails to harvest the resources in the environment.
- A lack of trustworthiness cannot depend on others in executing decisions.
- A lack of discipline fails to persist in executing decisions.

11. A leader who has an excess of these characteristics also makes bad decisions. These excesses lead to a completely different set of weaknesses. (4.7.1 Command Weaknesses).

- An excess of caring is too rigid in ideology to join with others.
- An excess of courage results in foolhardy decision making.
- An excess of knowledge creates paralysis from analysis.
- An excess of trustworthiness makes us too particular about satisfying others.
- An excess of discipline loses flexibility in responding to events.

Illustration:

The following principles apply to the element of leadership command:

1. Command is the responsibility of the individual. Any organization, such as the UN, which has no clear leader cannot be effective.

2. We are in command when we are making decisions for ourselves. The less free people are to make their own decisions, the less productive their lives will be.

3. The more successful we are at making decisions, the more people turn to us as a leader. President Obama was elected because he was able to make better decisions than his opponents through the course of the campaign, winning more and more support as time went on.

4. *As leaders, we must make decisions whether we want to or not.* When a leader tries to delegate the hard decisions, as we are seeing with President Obama on healthcare, he is increasingly seen as ineffective and weak and loses support.

5. *Command makes decisions to respond to events.* When a leader flounders in the face of events, as John McCain did in the face of the financial crisis at the end of the campaign, they lose support.

6. *Leaders must know which strategic areas require foresight and analysis*. When a leader cannot produce a cohesive picture of a situation, as President Bush failed to do in Iraq, they lose support.

7. *Leaders must train their subconscious minds for snap decision-making.* On September, 11, 2001, when Rudy Guiliani was faced with dealing with the attack on the World Trade Center, he made a number of good decisions without good information, saving thousands of lives.

8. *Small command decisions have the biggest impact on our lives over time.* While it is the dramatic public events that get all the media, people such as Norman Borlaug, the promoter of high yield crops in the developing world saved more lives than any single man in history, winning the Nobel Peace Prize in 1970 for his contributions.

9. *Leadership requires five qualities of character.* All presidents has these characteristics in one degree or another or they would not have risen to the top political post in the nation.

10. *A lack of character qualities in a leader, show up in five different ways*. Neville Chamberlain's relative lack of courage compared with Hitler lead to WWII.

11. *A leader who has an excess of these characteristics also makes bad decisions.* Hitler's excess of courage led to the destruction of Germany.

1.5.2. Group Methods

Sun Tzu's ten key methods regarding systems for executing decisions (skills).

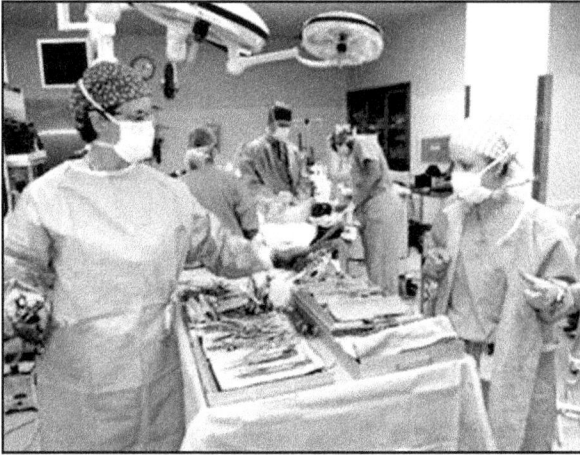

"Finally, you have your military methods. They shape your organization.
They come from your organization philosophy."
                              Sun Tzu's The Art of War 1:1:30-32

"An empowered organization is one in which individuals have the knowledge, skill, desire, and opportunity to personally succeed in a way that leads to collective organizational success."
                              Stephen Covey

General Principle: Methods of working with others are required to execute our decisions.

Situation:

Our decisions have no value until they are executed. If we decide to build a perpetual motion machine, the decision is meaningless. The task may seem desirable, but it is impossible. Decisions that cannot be executed by known methods are worse than worthless. Deciding to do something requires the knowledge that it can be done and an idea of how. As is so often the case with Sun Tzu, he sees this as a problem with understanding our boundaries and limitations. We can only accomplish what nature allows. The skills of any individual are limited. If we want to make valuable decisions, we must understand the chain of events that create value in our interactions with others. Knowing how to accomplish tasks starts with the challenge of finding the people who have the different types of knowledge we need. We can do little or nothing by ourselves.

Opportunity:

How well we execute our decisions depends on our methods. Methods describes both individuals skills and organizational systems. Sun Tzu's book is called "*The Art of War*," but Sun Tzu didn't use the word "art." His title for his work was *Bing-Fa*. The term *fa* means methods, skills, and systems. His first emphasis is on mastering a known set of skills. Mastery requires practice. Mastering Sun Tzu's strategy means practicing methods and procedures that are known to work in competitive situations. We instantly make better decisions when we choose actions based on existing skills. Since we have limited skills ourselves, we are more capable when, instead of trying to do everything ourselves, we combine our skills with others.

Key Methods:

The following ten key methods define the nature of the methods that allow us to execute our decisions.

1. Our methods include all our capabilities to execute decisions. Methods include all the skills, systems, and procedures that we use to transform our decisions into action. These skills include what we can do ourselves and our ability to connect with others who have complementary skills. These skills come from our knowledge. Our skills represent what we know about the laws of nature and using the resources in our environment. This knowledge first exists in our heads but we put it in our procedures and machines. We can leverage our environment only in the ways that it allows (2.6 Knowledge Leverage).

2. All individuals gain skills as they grow. Individuals develop skills based upon their unique experiences and their unique position. No one except that individual really knows the extent and limits of his or her skills and experience (1.9.2 Span of Control).

3. Our methods connect our position to the positions of others. Skills and the positions based on them exists only within the larger competitive landscape. Our competitive and productive skills are not developed or used in a vacuum. They are based on the resources the we get from our landscape, that is, from those around us. In this world of interconnections, our skills are compared with the skills of others as a part of our position. To improve our position, our actions must, by definition, affect our relationship with others in either an objective or subjective way (1.2 Subobjective Positions).

4. The most efficient methods divide tasks to develop individual expertise and group efficiencies. Leadership is the realm of the individual decisions, but methods are the realm of the division of labor. Our decisions don't produce value unless we work with other people to execute them in the least costly way. This execution depends on our ability to work with others. We organize to develop interconnected systems and procedures to get tasks done. In other words, we create organizations. Some of these systems rely on hiring individuals with personal skills and know-how, but many of these systems are built on organizational knowledge that is passed from one worker to the another (7.2.1 Proven Methods).

5. All individuals and organizations are unique in terms of their particular knowledge and abilities. Every person and organization has different skills and abilities. While many skill sets overlap, every set of skills is specialized in some way to fit the unique position of the individual and organization (1.1 Position Paths).

6. Methods are embodied in our established procedures, tools, and machinery. Skills don't only exist in the human mind and body. They also exist in the machines and tools that we developed to accomplish a set of tasks. The knowledge about how to accomplish that task is given physical form in the machine or tool. Each component is designed to accomplish a part of the task (7.3.1 Expected Elements).

7. *The methods we use must be consistent with our goals.* We use our skills, systems, and machines to attain a specific set of goals so we cannot use methods that, while they accomplish a limited purpose, damage our ability to satisfy the larger mission (1.6.3 Shifting Priorities).

8. *Successful methods are copied by others.* We copy the best practices of others to improve our methods. Others copy our best practices to improve their methods (1.8.1 Creation and Destruction).

9. *Methods must be continuously improved by innovation.* Innovation is a major component of good strategy. We make decisions based upon new information and we improve our methods by implementing innovations. These innovations can come from internal sources or copied from external sources (7.1.3 Standards and Innovation).

10. *Both competitive methods and production methods are necessary for strategy.* Productive methods are the skills by which we produce the most value for others from the resources that we control. Competitive methods are the skills with which we position ourselves against competitors to win the control of more resources (1.9 Competition and Production).

Illustration:

Below we offer various examples to help illustrate these principles.

1. *Our methods include all our capabilities to execute decisions.* Our abilities start with knowing how to speak a language, use our hands and feet, and get desired reactions from others.

2. *All individuals gain skills as they grow.* We start as babies with limited control over our bodies. As we grow, we develop certain common skills, such as walking and talking, but our unique

position and experiences determines the specific skills we develop, such as what language we speak.

*3. **Our methods connect our position to the positions of others.*** We contact people at the grocery store because we need groceries. We connect to customers because we want to sell our products. While I can write a book alone, I need what others have already made (a computer, paper, pen, etc.). in order to do it. I also need their future efforts. Writing the book has no value unless it is manufactured, distributed, and sold.

4. ***The most efficient methods divide tasks to develop individual expertise and group efficiencies.*** Both McDonald's restaurants and the Mayo Clinic develop systems for the tasks they need to accomplish. Every type of organization has a different type of methods.

*5. **All individuals and organizations are unique in terms of their particular knowledge and abilities***. A McDonald's restaurant doesn't have the same practices as a Burger King, but two McDonald's restaurants, no matter how similar, will operate differently because they employ different people with different skills who naturally balance their abilities. Each one of us is a unique constellation of skills gained from our unique path of experience.

*6. **Methods are embodied in our established procedures, tools, and machinery.*** A crowbar embodies a different form of knowledge than a computer but if the situation requires a crowbar, a computer won't do us much good.

*7. **The methods we use must be consistent with our goals.*** The simplest example is economic, we cannot waste money if we want to make money, but the most common example is moral: we cannot destroy people in order to save them. One of the most horrible examples are those who, in order to "save" people from the effects of DDT, condemned millions of poor, black children in Africa to death.

*8. **Successful methods are copied by others***. Globalization is the current word we use for the spread of manufacturing methods throughout the world.

9. *Methods must be continuously improved by innovation*. The quality and variety of food at McDonald's is better today than it was fifty years ago and will be better ten years from now than it is today.

10. *Both competitive methods and production methods are necessary for strategy*. The competition of an election produces a winning politician or political party, but unless those winners are able to convert their election into better lives for their citizens, they will be replaced, one way or another.

1.6.0 Mission Values

Sun Tzu's eight key methods about the goals and values needed for motivation.

"It starts with your philosophy.
Command your people in a way that gives them a higher shared purpose."

Sun Tzu's The Art of War 1:1:14-15

"The major reason for setting a goal is for what it makes of you to accomplish it. What it makes of you will always be the far greater value than what you get."

Jim Rohn

General Principle: Mission describes the motivations directing decisions and actions.

Situation:

We all have plenty of desires, but they change constantly and are often conflicting. Out of these conflicting desires comes our motivations, or what we call "mission" in Sun Tzu's strategy. An extremely common source of strategic mistakes is our failure to identify and clarify motivations. There are a whole list of problems associated with the lack of a clear mission. Without a clear mission, we drift with the situation at the mercy of our environment. We can react to events against our values and goals. Without understanding values and motivations, we will fail again and again in predicting people's behavior. Decisions and actions have no meaning outside of the context of goals and values that provide motivation.

If we don't understand motivations, we will get into trouble time and again without understanding why.

Opportunity:

The clearer our goals and priorities, the more likely we are to achieve them. If we don't know where we are going, any direction works as well. If we understand the motivations of others, we can work with them more effectively and predict their reactions (2.3.1 Action and Reaction). It is only our knowledge of goals and values that can change enemies into allies (1.5.1 Command Leadership). The better we understand values, our own and those of others, the easier it is for us to work together. Sun Tzu teaches that the best way to reach our own goals is to work with others in helping them reach theirs.

Key Methods:

These are the eight most important key methods that Sun Tzu offers regarding mission.

1. Mission is the central element of strategic position, connecting the other four key elements. The other four elements are the climate, ground, leader, and methods. In the original diagramming system of Chinese science and philosophy, the other four elements were the points in a compass and our goals were the center. Our mission defines the motivations that connect these elements and give them meaning. Our current position only has meaning in terms of our goals and values. The difference between our current position and desired position is defined by our mission. It is what gives our strategic position its direction (1.3 Elemental Analysis).

2. Our mission embodies our philosophy and our values in our goals. Sun Tzu defined mission as our shared, higher values. Mission is based on a belief system, that is, on a philosophy. Our goals encapsulate what we think is important. In an absolute sense, our mission captures both our purpose in life and the way that we think the world works. When Sun Tzu wrote about mission, he used the Chinese character *tao*, which is usually translated into English as "philosophy," but its literal meaning is "the path" (1.6.3 Shifting Priorities).

3. Everyone has a slightly different belief system based on their training and experience. Belief systems are highly complex. We can agree on many beliefs and still disagree on many others. People's unique combination of beliefs are based on their unique life experiences. No two people can live the same exact life because every path is unique (1.1 Position Paths).

4. All our individual goals and values are inherently self-centered. We can only see the world from our own, unique perspective. We only directly know our own thoughts and feelings. We value our beliefs because the are our own. Those who are willing to die for the one's they love are dying for their personal loves. Those who are willing to die for their beliefs are more dedicated to their personal vision than others. They believe that their physical life is less important than their ideal of self. Since everyone's beliefs are ultimately self-centered, disparaging anyone's goals as selfish is mere sophistry. The question is merely how many of our goals can we share with others (1.2 Subobjective Positions).

5. Our success depends on sharing our values with others. People can have goals and values that are completely selfish, but those goals and values are useless in terms of positioning. The important goals that create strength are those that can be shared. Organizations are impossible without a shared mission. The idea of a shared path captures many critical elements in creating a shared, higher mission. People can be on similar paths with different goals, just like people can share the same street going to different destinations. Everyone within an organization can have their own personal goals, but the organization's shared mission, values, and philosophy are the glue that holds those people together in a common business. Understanding the elements that can create a shared mission is critical to successful strategy (1.6.1 Shared Mission).

6. *All shared missions are limited.* Missions are always limited in scope of belief and often limited in time. We do not know or agree on the basis of a perfect Truth. We only agree on some limited aspects of our beliefs. If we think, "Everyone knows this is true," we are wrong. There is no such thing as a knowable and constant "common good." There are only temporary agreements about shared missions. At every point in human history, most things that everyone believed were eventually proven false. Much of what we believe today will be proven false eventually as well (2.1.1 Information Limits).

7. *Both creating allies and positioning against our rivals requires empathy.* Empathy is our capacity to see other people's mission from *their* perspective. We must get out of our own heads and into the mindframes of others. Without empathy, we cannot create winning positions. Empathy is the foundation of the warrior's creative mindset. If we cannot put ourselves into other people's shoes, we can never develop positions that win supporters. We cannot position against rivals unless we can predict their behavior by imagining what we would do in their positions. We must imagine both the range of possible values and changing priorities of both our potential supporters and opponents (1.6.3 Shifting Priorities).

8. *Roles such as ally and enemy are defined solely by mission interactions.* In its most abstract form, our *enemy* is any person whose mission conflicts with our own. An ally is someone with whom we share a mission. Positions that are complementary in one situation can compete in another situation (1.3.1 Competitive Comparison).

Illustration:

Let us illustrate these ideas discussing the general challenges of working in an organization with other coworkers.

1. Mission in the central element of strategic position, connecting the other four key elements. Everyone in the organization has a position. Each has their own ground (area), climate (attitudes), commands (decision-making), and methods (skills). All of these are united by each person's goals.

2. Our mission embodies our philosophy and our values in our goals. Everyone in an organization is working for their own individual goals.

3. Everyone has a slightly different belief system based on their training and experience. No matter how much we are like those with whom we work, it is our differences that create the strengths and weakness that make us better working together than apart.

4. All our individual goals and values are inherently self-centered. Each of us has an inflated sense of our own worth because only we know everything that we do. It is a trick of perspective. Closer things appear to be larger than things far away. We are all closer to ourselves.

5. Our success depends on sharing our values with others. We and our co-workers can share the "path" of making our company successful even though we may get different rewards from that success.

6. All shared missions are limited. Some will work for money, others for social approval, others to satisfy their own egos and so on. We can disagree about the right path to take both because our goals are different and because we see a different route as best. Agreement on goals does not mean agreement on means. What we all share at work is the belief that our organization is the best vehicle we have to satisfy our needs.

7. Both creating allies and positioning against our rivals requires empathy. We must understand what is important to those we work with. To motivate our co-workers more smoothly, we must put our needs in terms that address their missions.

8. Roles such as ally and enemy are defined solely by mission interactions. Our coworkers are our competition for internal promotions.

1.6.1 Shared Mission

Sun Tzu's ten key methods on finding goals that others can share.

"Trust only in yourself and the self-interest of others."
Sun Tzu's The Art of War 1:7:16

"If your imagination leads you to understand how quickly people grant your requests when those requests appeal to their self-interest, you can have practically anything you go after."

Napoleon Hill

General Principle: Higher values are the basis of shared missions that unite groups in powerful positions.

Situation:

When pushed, people push back. We cannot improve our position without the assistance of others, but everyone puts their own interests, goals, and opinions first. We cannot get people to commit to us unless we also make commitments to them. As Thomas Shelling said it in *The Strategy of Conflict*, "The power to constrain an adversary depends upon the power to bind oneself." People disagree about goals and values. Even when we agree on goals, we can disagree about methods and means. We can dissagree about where a given choice of path will lead. Even when we agree on means and ends, that agreement is often just temporary. Changes in climate shift a situation to create disagreement.

Opportunity:

Sun Tzu's strategy requires finding or constructing shared missions to bring people together as allies and supporters. Everyone's goals revolve around their own interests. Everyone is looking for friends, allies, and supporters.

People have an infinite number of desires. We can help them satisfy their own desires and in return they can help us toward our own goals, often unintentionally. Though people do often disagree about means and ends, there are a great many people in the world and their needs are constantly changing.

Opportunities exist in the short term, when we can temporarily agree on a means that suits our diverging goals. Opportunities exist in the long term. If we disagree on immediate actions, we still can always agree that the value of working together is greater and more certain than our differing opinions about actions.

Key Methods:

In constructing a shared mission, Sun Tzu provides the following key methods.

1. Shared missions are based on the current priorities that we have in common with others. When it comes to our personal mission, goals, and values, we all have a range of priorities. Shared missions are created by people who find common ground among those priorities. We can have areas of disagreement, but as long as our areas of agreement have a higher priority, we can create a shared mission. This higher priority is part of what Sun Tzu means by a "higher, shared purpose" (1.6.3 Shifting Priorities).

2. We must choose our methods based upon our shared mission. Tactics are the methods we choose to pursue our goal or mission. These methods can be based upon what is immediately convenient. They can bring people with different long-term missions together. Strategy requires a mission whose values are broad enough to share and enduring enough to persist (1.5.2. Group Methods).

3. A shared mission allows us to work with others to satisfy our mutual self-interest. In the original Chinese, the word Sun Tzu used to describe mission means literally "the way" or "the path." When we have serious disagreements over these means, we cannot find a shared mission even if we agree on all goals. The idea of means goes deeply into our philosophy of how the world works (1.6 Mission Values).

4. The depth of a mission determines how long alliances last. Without higher, longer-term goals, alliances will not hold. A group can never steer a consistent course and make any progress if they don't agree generally on direction. Without shared values, we cannot work with others, which makes success impossible (1.6 Mission Values).

5. We must avoid confusing a temporarily shared means for a shared longer-term mission. There is a difference between a tactical alliance of sharing the same means to different ends and a strategic one of sharing the same ends. Choosing the same path doesn't *always* mean a shared long-term goal. People can choose *some* of the same goals and *some* of the same parts of a path, working for mutual self-interest in some areas while competing in others. Our information about goals is never certain (2.1.1 Information Limits).

6. Trust arises when our actions demonstrate a priority on the shared values of the group. If everyone expects everyone else to stab them in the back at the earliest convenience, we cannot forge meaningful alliances. To create a high-trust group, we must visibly sacrifice our immediate self interest to those of the group. Such sacrifices occur naturally when our mutual self-interest depends upon each other. (2.3 Personal Interactions).

7. We can have the same general values but disagree on the best path to take. Shared values do not automatically create a shared mission. If people choose different paths, they cannot work together, helping each other along the way ((1.1 Position Paths).

8. Alliances based on shared values are not always possible. It is a mistake to think that we can always find common ground. There are goals that are absolutely diametrically opposed, where no shared means are possible simply because those goals lead in such different directions. Trusting in shared values without a demonstration of them gives people an invitation to deceive us (2.1.3 Misinformation and Disinformation

9. Empathy is the difference between selfishness and self-interest. The most obvious sign of the inability to find shared mission is a lack of empathy and understanding regarding differences in values and mission. Selfish values and goals leave no room for sympathy and empathy for those with different goals (1.6.2 Types of Motivations).

10. It takes creativity and perspective to construct shared goals to explore opportunities. Sun Tzu's system of innovation requires changing the order of things. We can do this by changing people's perception of the value of sharing a mission (7.3 Strategic Innovation).

Illustration:

Let us illustrate these principles with examples from a variety of areas.

1. Shared missions are based on the current priorities that we have in common with others. A good example is working with our coworkers in an organization. In an organization, our short-term opportunity comes from a shared mission with others who almost certainly have very different longterm goals. Some of us may be working simply for a weekly paycheck, while others are working to develop certain skills, while still others are working because they love the product the organization offers.

2. *We must choose our methods based upon our shared mission*. We use the methods of our organization, whether it is selling a product or converting people to a way of thinking, based upon the shared mission of the organization, not our individual goals.

3. *A shared mission allows us to work with others to satisfy our mutual self-interest.* Our differences in career direction over the long-term is less important than our agreement on the short term path. People within the same organization can have very different career paths over their lifetimes but work well together for the time they share the organization's goals.

4. *The depth of a mission determines how long alliances last.* The best example of our long-term opportunity is marriage. As two people in a marriage, we can agree the the value of our working together is greater and more certain than our differing opinions about the future.

5. *We must avoid confusing a temporarily shared means for a shared longer-term mission.* We can easily find a shared mission with those who have different goals. One person can join a company simply for the paycheck. Another can join for the professional experience. A third can join because of his or her personal relationship. However, all three of these people can work together because the mission of the company satisfies their different goals, at least for a period of time.

6. *Trust arises when our actions demonstrate a priority on the shared values of the group*. We all almost automatically sacrifice or our personal freedom to conform to certain social agreements. These agreements range from the use of money to the ban on public nudity. By our conformance, we earn the trust of others. Violating such agreements, in major ways, such as not paying our bills, destroys that trust. Even minor violations in our visible choices, such as a poor choice of clothing, undermines that trust.

7. *We can have the same general values but disagree on the best path to take*. For example, two opposing political parties can always agree on certain goals: reducing crime, poverty, improving health, and so on, but they cannot come to share a mission unless they can find some means to reach that goal that they can agree upon. Usually, one political party sees the other party's solutions as making the problem worse, not better. This is because of different views of how the world works.

8. *Alliances based on shared values are not always possible.* The classic historical mistake was Chamberlain's agreement with Hitler before WWII that was supposed to prevent war. It assumed that the two leaders agreed on the importance of avoiding the destruction of conflict.

9. *Empathy is the difference between selfishness and self-interest.* For example, religious extremists, including environmental extremists, are selfish because they cannot accept that others have the same right to opinions and choices that they do. Such extremists not only see their beliefs as the only acceptable beliefs, but they feel the need to force everyone to live by their rules. This requires not only putting their opinions above the opinions of others, but a belief that others must not be free to make their own decisions.

10. *It takes creativity and perspective to construct shared goals to explore opportunities.* A common method is to exaggerate the danger of a common enemy.

1.6.2 Types of Motivations

Sun Tzu's six key methods regarding hierarchies of motivation that define missions.

"You can exploit five different needs in a leader. If he is willing to die, you can kill him.
If he wants to survive, you can capture him.
He may have a quick temper.
You can then provoke him with insults.
If he has a delicate sense of honor, you can disgrace him.
If he loves his people, you can create problems for him."
Sun Tzu's The Art of War 8:5:1

"Motivation is the art of getting people to do what you want them to do because they want to do it."
Dwight David Eisenhower

General Principle: Five levels of mission form unique individual motivations.

Situation:

Sun Tzu teaches us to leverage people's motivations, but that can be a challenge. Everyone has a constellation of sometimes competing goals and values inside their head. One of the most challenging strategic problems is trying to understand what other people want. Sun Tzu's system is *allocentric*. This means that it focuses on the interests and concerns of others. We use their interests to further our own. The problem, of course, is that human beings in general have a complex array of motives, and each person is unique. Not only that, but their motivations can change from moment to moment as the situation changes. So the problem gets worse when we try to predict the interests of others in the future. Some motives are very changeable while others are more stable.

Opportunity:

Sun Tzu teaches us not to worry about understanding people perfectly. Our goal is only to understand the motives of others a little more clearly than most people do. Remember, in using Sun Tzu's principles, it is only our relative superiority of position that counts (1.3.1 Competitive Comparison). Sun Tzu model for motivation stresses 1) the external focus, 2) simplicity, and 3) interconnections to the other elements of his system. The external focus is important because most people are too preoccupied with their own wants and needs. The practice of strategy forces us to get out of ourselves and see the world from the perspective of others. Simplifying motivations is critical because human beings are unbelievably complex and we need a practical system. We handle this complexity by interconnecting motivations to every part of Sun Tzu's system. This perspective is so valuable that it is one of the nine major categories of strategic knowledge (2.0 Developing Perspective).

Key Methods: The six key methods that define different types of motivation are described below.

1. People's motives connect to every element of their strategic positions. All five elements act as our reference points for motivations. This system was designed to simplify the questions that we ask about people's motivations. It focuses on the motivations that we can use to make decisions in a well-defined way. Other systems, such as Maslow's hierarchy of needs, which Sun Tzu's system strongly resembles, have categories, such as "self actualization," that can neither be compared nor shared. This makes them difficult to use in strategic decisions (1.3 Elemental Analysis).

2. Our desire for meaning is based on our belief in ultimate goals and eternal values. This is the highest, deepest, and rarest form of motivation. We sometimes refer to them as "spiritual" missions. These are the missions for which people are willing to die, which is how Sun Tzu refers to them above. They are based on our very specific ideas of the meaning of life and how the world works. Because of the deep level of importance people attach to these motivations, shared spiritual missions can create organizations that last for millennia. We can kill the people, but not the mission. Spiritual or philosophical motives connect with the core of mission (1.6 Mission Values).

3. Our desire for survival arises from our physical and economic needs. This basic or "ground" level of motivation. It is the most common and predictable level of mission. We must meet our physical needs simply to survive. By "economic," we mean whatever we need to survive and thrive: food, shelter and our possessions. Money, of course, can get us any of these. This is the broadest level of mission. We all share the need to physically survive. Physical motives connect to Ground ((1.4.2 Ground Features).

4. The desire for predictability arises from our need for safety in dealing with change. We want to feel secure from unpredictable threats. The importance of predictability rises and falls with the changing cycles in the environments. As conditions worsen and become more unpredictable, safety becomes more important. Climate takes the subjective form of our basic emotions concerning the future. If we are worried and anxious about the future, we react with fear or anger. If we are secure and confident in the future, we are optimistic and relaxed. Safety motives connect to Climate (2.4.2 Climate Perspective).

5. The desire for control arises from our need for respect and authority. These are our motivations for individual recognition, attention, and social status. We can describe these motivations as either "social" or "personal" since they involve our desire for social recognition of our individual qualities of character. This reputation is the basis for our credibility, especially our professional position. The more recognition and respect we receive, the more authority we are given by society. The result is more individual command over our lives. These desires are as common as our physical desires, but their importance depends on our individual character. Personal motives connect to the key element of command (1.5.1 Command Leadership).

6. The desire for relationships arises from our need for belonging and friendship. This motivation comes from our membership in a group, a team, or a marriage rather than our individual social reputation. Our membership in these relationships gives us personal meaning through our interconnections with others. These personal relationships are deeper than our social status. The relationships are more intimate and direct than our general social status. All motivations relate to emotion, but here we are really talking about the giving and receiving of love. These missions are the narrowest, exclusive to our circle of close relationships, i.e. friends and family, but they are very deep and important to us. Since these motives are defined by our interdependence on others, they connect to the key element of methods (1.5.2. Group Methods).

Illustration:

Different organizations exist to satisfy one of these levels of motivation. One of the most common mistakes we see in the organizations that we work with is that they lose track of their mission.

1. **People's motives connect to every element of their strategic positions.** A given person has motivations at all these levels, so they usually have positions in many different arenas in order to satisfy them.

2. **Our desire for meaning is based on our belief in ultimate goals and eternal values.** Churches, social movements, political parties, and all other religious organizations work at this level.

3. Our desire for survival arises from our physical and economic needs. Businesses that provide food, clothing, housing, and financial services all serve this level.

4. ***The desire for predictability arises from our need for safety in dealing with change.*** Political organizations exist to provide basic levels of security and safety.

5. ***The desire for control arises from our need for respect and authority.*** Every type of organization and professional association that recognizes authority and professionalism addresses this level of motivation.

6. ***The desire for relationships arises from our need for belonging and friendship.*** The family is the most basic organization here providing relationships, but the personal emotional connections can arise among people in any other type of group.

1.6.3 Shifting Priorities

Sun Tzu seven key methods about how missions change according to temporary conditions.

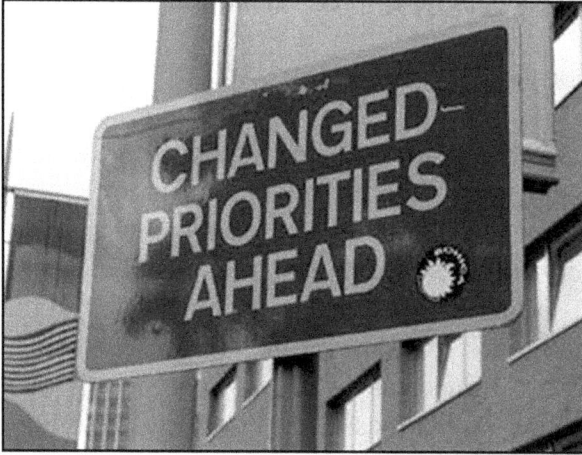

"You must predict the enemy to overpower him and win."
Sun Tzu's The Art of War 10:3:3

"Goals are simply tools to focus your energy in positive directions, these can be changed as your priorities change, new ones added, and others dropped."
O. Carl Simonton

General Principle: Changing conditions not fixed goal posts determine current mission priorities.

Situation:

People's motivation changes over time, both gradually and suddenly. Our goals and values change their relative importance depending upon our situation. For example, our long-term goals are suddenly very unimportant when we find ourselves in a life-or-death situation. Since strategy depends on predicting what others will do, this complex array of desires makes prediction difficult as it changes from moment to moment. We can never perfectly predict people's behavior because we can never understand exactly what is motivating them at the moment. This means that there are limits to how much we can depend on our alliance. Over time, allies can actually become enemies, depending on the situation. Most partnerships fall apart because our interests naturally diverge over time.

Opportunity:

Our mission *as a whole* is the most enduring part of our strategic positions (1.6 Mission Values). Sun Tzu's strategy gives us an easy-to-see system for understanding the hierarchy of motivations that relates to everything else we know about positions (1.6.2 Types of Motivations). While the specific order of priorities on this list can change from moment to moment, the list as a whole changes very slowly if at all. This hierarchy also tells us generally how the five different types of motivations tend to change over time, which are more temporary and which are longer lasting. This gives us a critical head start in terms of predicting the choices that people will make. We combine this understanding with another key aspect of our strategic model, knowing how changing conditions affect positions ((1.4.1 Climate Shift).

Key Methods:

There are many different levels to mission. Each person has their own private constellation of values and desires within a general framework. In everyday life, we can think of some of our goals as short-term and others as long-term, but we base much of our interaction with others upon knowing which of their motivations we can predict and which we cannot.

1. The priorities of our mission change as conditions change. This include both conditions in the external environment (1.4 The External Environment) and conditions within a person or organization (1.5 Internal Elements).

2. Both predictable and unpredictable changes in conditions affect motives. This means some changes in priorities will be predictable but others will not. (2.3.2 Reaction Unpredictability).

3. The most regular changes in priorities come from our cycle of internal needs and appetites. There is a natural cycle in our competing desires. The lowest levels of motivations are the most temporary because we know what our physical needs require and how we need to address them (1.8.3 Cycle Time).

4. Other predictable changes are linked to external cycles of climate. The external environment can also be predictable in its effect upon our priorities. We categorize these changes under climate, both the physical, social, and business climates (1.4.1 Climate Shift).

5. *These changes are predictable because they are linked to the external passage of time.* Whether we are looking at ourselves or others, we can understand that at certain times of day or year, we need to address different sets of needs (3.1.6 Time Limitations).

6. Unpredictable, non-cyclic internal and external events also affect priorities. These events can offer us either unexpected opportunities or unexpected problems. In either case, we must change our immediate priorities in order to address them (3.2 Opportunity Creation).

7. Knowing the events that affect others gives us insight into their current priorities. When we cannot predict changes in priorities, we must immediately adapt our viewpoint based on our knowledge of events. People cannot do everything at once and must change their priorities in order to address events (3.1.1 Resource Limitations).

Illustration:

Let us look at some simple examples of how priorities change in each of these categories.

1. The priorities of our mission change as conditions change. No matter how much more important our professional goals are over the long term, we must take time every day to eat and sleep to address our physical needs.

2. Both predictable and unpredictable changes in conditions affect motives. We can predict when we will get sleepy but not when we will get ill.

3. The most regular changes in priorities come from our cycle of internal needs and appetites. We will get hungry every day and sleepy every night.

4. Other predictable changes are linked to external cycles in the climate. For example, most of us work on economic and professional needs during the day because that is when we traditionally do business. Our emotional mission is more often addressed in the evening or on weekends. During summer, we take vacation. Certain business climate changes, such as Christmas shopping, are also predictable. At tax time, we will pay our taxes.

5. These changes are predictable because they are linked to the external passage of time. Day and night, winter and summer, taxes, and human aging are all predictable.

6. Unpredictable, non-cyclic internal and external events also affect priorities. We can get sick. An economic collapse in an industry can arise.

7. Knowing the events that affect others gives us insight into their current priorities. If we know someone has lost a lot of money, we can expect that they will focus more on activities relating to immediately raising money.

1.7.0 Competitive Power

Sun Tzu's ten key methods describing the sources of superiority in challenges.

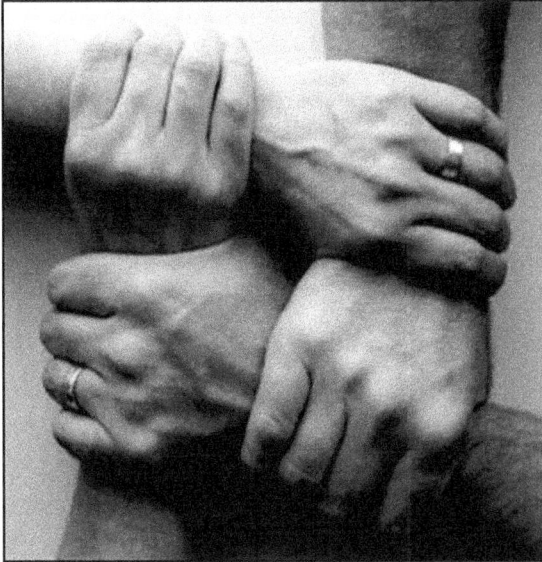

"Manage to avoid battle until your organization can count on certain victory. You must calculate many advantages."

Sun Tzu's The Art of War 1:5:1-2

"Build for your team a feeling of oneness, of dependence on one another and of strength to be derived by unity."

Vince Lombardi

General Principle: Strategic power comes from unity and focus, not size or the wealth of resources.

Situation:

How we determine if one strategic position is superior to another? How do we predict which strategic position will triumph in a comparison with competing positions? Our expectations are often very wrong. We expect larger organizations to be successful. We also expect organizations that have been successful in the past to continue to be successful in the future. We also expect the volume of resources used to have an impact. The problem is that these factors have very little effect on competitive outcomes. Size and wealth are the result of past success, but that success may have little relationship with the current mission. Sun Tzu teaches that size is not power and that past success is not momentum. In the real world, smaller forces often triumph over larger ones. Newer organizations often overcome established ones. Vast resources are often squandered in failed endeavors. This meant that something deeper was going on, something that isn't obvious to most of us without training.

Opportunity:

Sun Tzu developed his strategic system in part to explain our misconceptions about strength. Once we understand what a "strategic advantage" really means, we can predict which battles we will win and which we will lose. More importantly, we will stop wasting our efforts in areas that create as many disadvantages as advantages. This includes the size of an organization (3.4 Dis-Economies of Scale), past success (3.2.5 Dynamic Reversal), and expending resources (3.1.1 Resource Limitations).

Key Methods: The following ten key methods describe Sun Tzu's concept of competitive power.

Power means our capacity to move to a superior position despite meeting challenges and obstacles. Power is only required to overcome opposing conditions in our external environment.

1. When the opposing conditions come from the opposition of rivals, power is a relative comparison of the capacities of each party to move against another. Power is specifically the ability to advance a position toward a goal, as opposed to simply defending an existing position (1.1 Position Paths).

*2. **Power gives rise to relative strength of position in compari-son to other positions**. Strength comes from superior resources gained from controlling a given position, but it exists only as a comparison with other competing positions. There are many different types of strength, but all forms of strength are relative, arising from a comparison among potential alternatives and contesting positions. That comparison is based upon only a single criteria: the ability to a position to fulfill our mission of moving toward a goal. In making this comparison, some positions have advantages over others. An "advantage" can mean many different things in different situations, but all of them had to relate directly to supporting the mission. This realization lead Sun Tzu to develop a new idea about what the term "strength" really means in succeeding at a challenge (<u>1.3.1 Competitive Comparison</u>).

*3. **Strategic power arises from the unity and focus that comes from mission.** Unity creates focus. Focus creates strength. Unity and focus together define all the advantages that can come from a strategic position in order to create strength (<u>1.6 Mission Values</u>).

*4. **Power is created when people focus their energy and other resources at a single place at a single time.** This requires us to use the shape of the terrain since we all must be in contact with the focus point. We must have an opening in the shifts of climate to make it possible for everyone to act together at one time (<u>1.4.1 Climate Shift</u>).

*5. **The smaller the focus point in time and space, the greater the power.** Intense efforts cannot last long so they must be kept short. Impact is dissipated over too much space (5.5 Focused Power).

*6. **Power is amplified when focused on relative weakness.** We use the term "strength" to describe the advantage that results from targeting weaknesses. The weakness of the target emphasizes the relative power of the move (3.2.4 Emptiness and Fullness).

*7. **Power requires a leader clearly articulating the target, the direction, and the timing.** Advantages come from a leader having the vision and communication skills necessary to rally supporters around the mission focusing on a single goal (1.5.1 Command Leadership).

8. Power requires methods that move people together at the same time. Good methods offer an advantage because they keep everyone together, focusing them on the goal. Disadvantageous methods create division, limiting focus to individual separate tasks rather than progress toward shared goals (1.5.2. Group Methods).

9. Every existing organization represents a formula of unity and focus. All success is built around using these aspects of power. An organization's formula addresses conditions in its environment creating the focus, the intensity, the clarity, and the unity success requires. Large, successful organizations grow and advance their position when their formula works better than other competing formulas for addressing the same values and goals (1.5 Competing Agents).

10. Size, success and wealth are a result of power not its source. Organizations, no matter how large and successful, fail when their formulas, which may have worked in the past, lose their potency. Those organizations may be strong in terms of resources, but they are not powerful unless they can move to positions that advance their position. Though strong, large organizations easily lose their focus and mission. Their mission becomes diluted, spread-out, muddy, and divided, at least when compared with other alternative organizations. Their success formulas get outmoded and outdated. Formulas grow outdated when they no longer generate the unity and focus that they have in the past. Without unity and focus on fulfilling a shared mission, the elements that make up a group's strategic position are weakly connected (3.4 Dis-Economies of Scale).

Illustration:

Let us illustrate these principles in the simplest form possible, discussing power in the terms of slicing bread and rowing a boat.

1. Power means our capacity to move to a superior position despite meeting challenges and obstacles. A tool works because it helps us make a move to a superior position. When our goal is cut-ting a slice of bread, we want the power to smoothly separate one piece of bread from the loaf.

*2. **Power gives rise to relative strength of position in comparison to other positions**.* Strength is having the bread in a more usable form to satisfy a weakness, in this case, our hunger. The power of a knife allows us get those resources.

*3. **Strategic power arises from the unity and focus that comes from mission**.* It is the unity, that is the solidity of the knife, and its focus, that is its sharpness that gives it its power. A knife made of butter will not work. A knife with a dull blade also will not work.

4. ***Power is created when people focus their energy and other resources at a single place at a single time**.* The edge of the knife focusing the power of our hand in a very narrow area.

*5. **The smaller the focus point in time and space, the greater the power**.* A knife requires less force than a club because it focuses force in the smallest possible space.

*6. **Power is amplified when focused on relative weakness**.* A knife cuts a loaf of bread but it will not cut a bar of steel.

*7. **Power requires a leader clearly articulating the target, the direction, and the timing**.* Since we are now talking about a group of people, let us change our illustration to a boat manned by a crew rowing through the water. In rowing, the coxswain steers the boat and provides the tempo.

*8. **Power requires methods that move people together at the same time**.* If some people are pushing or dragging their oars, the group's focus, unity, and strength are lost.

*9. **Every existing organization represents a formula of unity and focus**.* Different rowing crews can use very different formulas. Some can concentrate on agile members and speed of the stroke while others can depend on more muscular members who use more forceful strokes.

*10. **Size, success and wealth are a result of power not its source**.* Any sports team that wins consistently will become larger in terms of its supporters and get better candidates, in terms of its formula for success for joining the team. However, this does not prevent better formulas using very different types of competitors from coming along and beating it. The larger and stronger a team gets, the more likely it is that a smaller, quicker team will eventually be able to beat it.

1.7.1 Team Unity

Sun Tzu's ten key methods for increasing our strength by the way we join with others.

Unity works because it enables you to win every battle you fight.

Sun Tzu's The Art of War 3:5:1

"Unity to be real must stand the severest strain without breaking."

Mahatma Gandhi

General Principle: The strength of a team's unity depends on leveraging individuality.

Situation:

What makes a team different than any random group of people? What should make it different is its unity, the internal bond that makes a group strong. Bringing a group together doesn't automatically create that bond. As easily as groups can come together, they also come apart. As humans, we have two opposing natures. Part of our nature is as social creatures. We are drawn into groups and look for group approval and support. However, we also have a strong drive toward individuality, and we are natural critics of the group. That side of our nature resists losing our identity to the group, forsaking the strength of the group for our own independence.

Opportunity:

The opportunity in unity for the individual comes from the strength of the group. Working with a group of people gives us access to broader skills and more resources than we have alone. The opportunity for the group is to bring people together in a way that their individuality strengthens rather than weakens the group. We can increase unity by celebrating individuality rather than suppressing it.

Key Methods:

Unity works when it brings a team together so that others want to join as well. A successful team makes the individual special, adding distinctiveness rather than subtracting it. While we can never win everyone over, if we win enough people, those that still oppose us will not attempt a direct meeting in competition. The strategy of unity encompasses a number of important concepts:

1. Unity increases if each person feels responsible for the group as a whole. When responsibility for the group as a whole is limited to management, the team will not be very unified. A team is unified when each individual feels responsible for the well-being of the group as a whole (1.7.2 Goal Focus).

2. Unity increases if individuals trust each other to handle their individual responsibilities. This means that each individual knows his or her area of responsibility, is capable of handling it, and is trusted by others in performing it (6.8.3 Individual Toughness).

3. Unity increases when individuals can work independently for the good of the team. External team processes are usually more disconnected than internal team processes. When the environment is controlled, unifying internal processes is easy. External activities are much more difficult to coordinate because the external environment is unpredictable and chaotic (1.9.2 Span of Control).

4. Unity increases when member's contributions are regularly recognized. The best programs recognize most people most of the time. This puts pressure on individual members who fail to contribute, making them more aware of their shortcomings even if the group itself doesn't make an issue of them (6.8.2 Group Strength).

5. Unity increases from acting together under external pressure. Shared danger, action, and success have a unifying power. Unity doesn't come from making speeches. Opposition creates unity because it can force a group to come together. Situations with less opportunity to act together and win battles together tend to pull organizations apart (9.3.1 Mutual Danger).

6. Unity increases if individuals have complementary strengths and weaknesses. Differences between individuals can increase unity more than similarity. Different personalities and skill sets depend on one another. Putting differences together in the right formula is the basis of strength in unity. A homogeneous group, where individuals have the same opinions and skills, will tend to agree on decisions, but it is limited in what it can do. A diverse group will tend to have broader perspective on a situation and more skills to apply to any given task, but it requires more trust in leadership to make decisions (3.5 Strength and Weakness).

7. Unity increases when the mission minimizes differences in individual goals. The construction of a common mission is often the most creative and important work in strategy. Individuals may belong to a group for very different reasons and have different goals, however, they must find a common goal in the mission of the group. The job of creating groups is largely the work of imagining shared missions (1.6.1 Shared Mission).

8. Unity increases when new members become the responsibility of existing individual members. Membership starts with direct personal relationships and responsibility. New members should feel responsible to their mentors and existing members should feel responsible to their wards (6.8 Competitive Psychology).

9. Unity increases with clear chains of command. Good leadership involves a number of issues. The three most important are 1) clear lines of authority, 2) decisions that can be executed given the situation, and 3) communication skills that unify people ((1.5.1 Command Leadership).

10. Unity increases when opponents are unable to exploit its natural divisions. Networked organizations with many connections between members are stronger than large organizations with clear divisions in the hierarchy that can be exploited (9.2.5 Vulnerability of Organization).

Illustration:

Some examples of how these principles are used or violated are below.

1. Unity increases if each person feels responsible for the group as a whole. A soldier's first priority is to the members of his or her unit.

2. Unity increases if individuals trust each other to handle their individual responsibilities. In NFL football, a defensive lineman can only defend his gap if he trusts his fellow linemen to defend their gaps.

3. Unity increases when individuals can work independently for the good of the team. Within most large sales organizations, there are constant conflicts between sales responsibilities among different territories and divisions but individuals are still able to work together.

4. Unity increases when member's contributions are regularly recognized. Most "employee of the month" programs are an example of too little, too seldom. Most people are always excluded so there is no pressure to perform.

5. Unity increases from acting together under external pressure. A dangerous common enemy has historically been the best glue holding together an alliance.

6. Unity increases if individuals have complementary strengths and weaknesses. Human beings have two separate physical forms: men and women. The oldest, more proven, and most successful team in human history, is a marriage based on uniting these differences.

7. Unity increases when the mission minimizes differences in individual goals. While golf is a great contest of individuals, team events, such as the President's cup, offer no individual awards. All proceeds going to charity.

8. Unity increases when new members become the responsibility of existing individual members. Groups that leave new members to find their own way lose most of their members.

9. Unity increases with clear chains of command. The reason that many ad hoc groups fail to accomplish their goals and fall apart is that responsibility is shared to the degree that it doesn't exist. Unity increases when opponents are unable to exploit its natural divisions. One of the reasons that American car companies ran into so many problems was that their divisions created internal politics and conflict.

10. Unity increases when opponents are unable to exploit its natural divisions. As organizations grow larger, internal separation in hierarchies create rival divisions who compete for resources within the organization.

1.7.2 Goal Focus

Five key methods regarding strength as arising from concentrating efforts.

"Where you focus, you unite your forces.
When the enemy divides, he creates many small groups."
Sun Tzu's The Art of War 3:5:1

"One reason so few of us achieve what we truly want is
that we never direct our focus; we never concentrate our
power. Most people dabble their way through life, never
deciding to master anything in particular."
Tony Robbins

General Principle: The strength of a team's focus depends on its concentration.

Situation:

Strategic strength depends on two characteristics: unity and focus. The problem is that from our ordinary, everyday perspective these qualities are opposite from one another. Most of us see unity as inclusive and focus as exclusive. To bring teams together, we must include other views, but to focus the team, we must exclude other views. The problem is that without both components, we cannot create strength. Unity without a sharp focus is weak. A sharp focus without unity behind it is also weak.

Opportunity:

Understanding competitive positions in terms of the five elements gives us a more specific and useful definition of unity and focus (1.3 Elemental Analysis). Our opportunity comes from clearly separating the external environment and the internal organization (1.4 The External Environment, 1.5 Internal Organization). Focus excludes most of the environment while including all of the organization. It works by concentrating group efforts in a very small external time and place.

Key Methods:

Focus enables easier decision-making because it eliminates what cannot be done given the limitations of space and time. If we know for certain what we should not do, it makes it easier to choose what we should do.

1. Creating focus requires recognizing limits. Our resources are inherently limited. Because our resources are limited, we cannot spread them too thinly. If we spread them too thinly, we create weakness relative to our competition. We cannot do everything and be everywhere at all times. Those that try to compete everywhere (ground) and do everything (methods) are weak everywhere in everything (3.1.1 Resource Limitations).

2. Creating focus requires concentration of resources. We limit the space and within that limited space we concentrate resources. If we concentrate many skills and resources in a limited space for a limited period of time, we create a competitive mismatch. In that place and time, you want to be in every way superior to your competition at the time of battle *(3.1.4 Openings)*.

3. *We use focus to create a mismatch at the focus point.* *Battle* in Sun Tzu's strategy is defined as simply meeting a competitor or a challenge. It doesn't mean destructive *conflict*, which is a distinct concept and very different Chinese character. If we create a mismatch of resources at the time of the competitive meeting, we will have all the advantages in that time and space (3.2.4 Emptiness and Fullness).

4. *Creating focus requires* a *limited mission.* The more generic the mission is, the more useless it is in terms of focus. The more specific a mission is, the easier it is to see if an action falls within the scope of that mission. Strategy recognizes the problem of ***mission creep. Mission creep*** is the tendency of missions to broaden over time, losing their focus and, therefore, their strength and power. Interestingly, a limited mission also often works to creating unity, but while focus works by limiting ground, unity works by limiting time. People can have different destinations, but they can still share a path for a limited period of time (1.6.3 Shifting Priorities).

5. *Creating focus over time is necessary to create persistence.* Persistence is another form of concentration, but it isn't the same as continuing what isn't working for a little longer. To find success, even in a limited area, we have to persistently adjust our efforts to find the right method for success. The key question is always how long do we persist before we realize that we are doing something wrong and make adjustments (5.5 Focused Power).

Illustration:

The best analogy for focus is starting a fire using a magnifying glass. Starting a fire requires:

1. Creating focus requires recognizing limits. We must concentrate the heat of the sun, our limited resources, which is insufficient for starting a fire if spread out.

2. Creating focus requires concentration of resources. We must concentrate that heat in the smallest possible area of fuel.

3. We use focus to create a mismatch at the focus point. We don't focus on what is hard to ignite, a piece of wood, but what is easy, paper or soft tinder.

4. Creating focus requires a *limited mission.* We only focus until we get the fire smoldering, then we must immediately switch to broader activities such as blowing and adding fuel.

5. Creating focus over time is necessary to create persistence. It will take several tries to start the fire, adjusting our methods, to get the right angle and distance, and holding the focus motionless long enough to be effective.

1.8.0 Progress Cycle

Sun Tzu's ten key methods regarding the adaptive loop by which positions are advanced.

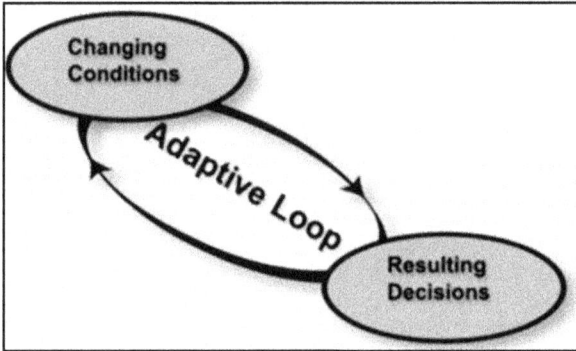

> *"End and yet return to start."*
> Sun Tzu's The Art of War 5:2:7 (literal translation of Chinese characters).

> *Failure is the opportunity to begin again, more intelligently."*
>
> Henry Ford

General Principle: Only a continuous loop of adapting to situations advances positions.

Situation:

Competitive processes are not linear. Production processes are linear. They convert raw materials step by step into a finished product. At the end of a production process, the product is finished. A linear process runs in one direction. The problem is that we are only trained in traditional schools for linear thinking, so we expect competitive processes to be linear, but they are not. They are cyclic. They continually loop back upon themselves, reincorporating feedback from the environment into our next choice of actions. Their processes are never finished. They have no true end point. Whether successful or not, each advance requires another advance. The process is always a loop. Every advance brings us back to the beginning where we start working on our next advance.

Opportunity:

Our opportunity is to embrace the loopy nature of strategy. This nature means that, though we never reach the end, we also can never truly fail. Each loop, whether it succeeds or fails, is a learning experience. Even if we fail to make the move we attempted, we still improve our position by learning more about our position and situation.

Key Methods:

1. The adaptive loop is the constant reaction to objective and subjective conditions in the environment. We take in information from the environment, make decisions, take actions, and establish positions. In the next cycle of the loop, we again adjust our information, decisions, actions and positions. In the first two stages, we work with subjective information, in the last two stages, with physical matters following the subjective and objective nature of positions (1.2 Subobjective Positions).

2. The adaptive loop is a two-part cycle of expansion and contraction. Like a beating heart or breathing, in half of the cycle we reach out to gather broadly from the environment then we narrow our focus by making decisions. We then open ourselves to events by taking action, then we narrow our focus again to establish a position. We can think of the expansion stage as the destruction of feeding off the environment and the contraction stage as the creation of something new in the environment (1.8.1 Creation and Destruction).

3. We call the adaptive loop the Progress Cycle because its only purpose is advancing a position. In its simplest form, we describe the adaptive loop as Listen > Aim > Move > Claim following the terms we developed in our most general work, *The Golden*

Key to Strategy. This short form is both easy to remember and easily applicable to a wide variety of areas. In The Playbook, we use a more sophisticated and detailed description of this cycle. This form was first developed in our work, *9 Formulas for Business Success*. In this form, understanding the nature of competitive positions sits at the center. The cycle itself is represented by the other formulas, breaking down Listen > Aim > Move > Claim into more detail: Listening to gather information to see positions more clearly (2.0 Developing Perspective).

4. The Progress Cycle starts with listening to put together a big picture to see openings. This is where we reach out into the environment. We open ourselves to the nature of the situation with the specific goal of seeing where we need to move (3.0 Identifying Opportunities).

5. The Progress Cycle requires aiming at only the opportunities that are the most likely to be successful. Unlike the productive moves of linear planning, we do not know exactly what will happen in any competitive move. Because our resources are limited, we must prioritize the opportunities that we explore, choosing those that are the most likely to be successful. (4.0 Leveraging Probability).

6. The Progress Cycle then aims at minimizing our mistakes. To explore new areas more successfully, we are going to make mistakes because success is only a probability. Many attempts will fail. We must learn how to handle those failures so they do not eliminate future success. (5.0 Minimizing Mistakes).

7. The Progress Cycle then acts, moving in standard ways to meet the challenges of the opportunity. This is the first component of the move part of the cycle. It is expansive, since our actions must move out of areas we control into new areas. In those areas, we must respond to situations in the ways that have proven to be the most effective in the past (6.0 Situation Response).

8. The Progress Cycle completes moves through creativity. While standard responses help us meet the challenges of the situation, we create the momentum we need to succeed only through creativity. This is the focusing stage of the moving cycle (7.0 Creating Momentum).

9. The Progress Cycle wins rewards by claiming them. Sun Tzu teaches that the rewards of a position must be claimed. This expansion stage again reaches out into the environment, in this case, for the benefits of the position to which we have moved (8.0 Winning Rewards).

10. The Progress Cycle claims rewards in order to defend our gains. This is the concentration stage, where we use the productivity of a position to secure it (9.0 Using Vulnerability).

Illustration:

1. The adaptive loop is the constant reaction to objective and subjective conditions in the environment. None of us are inventing this cycle. It exists in nature. Our job as scientists is simply to describe it so that people can recognize what is happening and use this knowledge for their own purposes. Once we understand the adaptive loop, we easily recognize its use in every form of competition.

2. The adaptive loop is a two-part cycle of expansion and contraction. The cycle is a feedback loop, continuously correcting our course as we navigate the environment. This cycle is scalable. For example, in sales, the large scale loop is often described as "qualification," "presentation," "overcoming objections," and "closing." Properly understood, this maps directly to Sun Tzu's description of "to learn," "to aim," "to march," and "to form."

3. *We call the adaptive loop the Progress Cycle because its only purpose is advancing a position.* Each "step" of the loop has within it smaller feedback loops. In military competition, recognizing the adaptive loop is a matter of life and death. 2,500 years ago, Sun Tzu in *The Art of War* described the cycle most generally as "to learn," "to see," "to march," and "to form." As a general, his focus was on the large scale movement of troops that took days or weeks. In other eras where different weapons and actions come into

play, strategists always see the complete cycle, but focused on different parts. In the 20th century, Col. John Boyd, saw the first part of the cycle as more important, He described the whole cycle as "to observe," "to orient," "to decide," and "to act," the OODA loop. As a fighter pilot, his interest was on loops that lasted a few seconds.

*4. **The Progress Cycle starts with listening to put together a big picture to see openings.*** For example, when we are in a period of gathering information, we are still acting, asking questions.

*5. **The Progress Cycle requires aiming at only the opportunities that are the most likely to be successful**.* There are hundreds of other competitive arenas where the adaptive loop is described in the specific language of the profession or the activity. Product design, political campaigns, military campaigns, sports events, and every other field in which people endeavor to improve their position have their own language for describing their version of the adaptive loop.

*6. **The Progress Cycle then aims at minimizing our mistakes**.* In military battles, we must preserve our army. In sports contests, we must keep the score close. In product design, we cannot create products that are too expensive to build.

*7. **The Progress Cycle then acts, moving in standard ways to meet the challenges of the opportunity**.* Every competitive arena has its own standard methods for dealing with different situations, but those methods are standards because they usually work.

*8. **The Progress Cycle completes moves through creativity**.* Those who succeed in every competitive arena are those that go beyond the standard to invent new responses. These responses are not merely superior execution of what is expected but a change from what is expected to what creates surprise.

*9. **The Progress Cycle wins rewards by claiming them**.* These feedback loops can take weeks or months or even years. For example, designing a new product and bringing it to market. But within these long loops are many little loops, some of which last only a few seconds. The cycle is only complete when the reward or benefit of the move is converted from potential to reality. Money is made. Opponents surrender the field.

10. The Progress Cycle claims rewards in order to defend our gains. When we win rewards, we set up a reason for others to want to take them from us. We now have a position to defend, so we must consider our vulnerabilities. Defending a position is easier than winning it, but it cannot be over looked. This defense, however, is also the basis for a new cycle of advancing our position.

1.8.1 Creation and Destruction

Sun Tzu's five key methods on the creation and destruction of competitive positions.

"It is the basis of life and death.
It is the philosophy of survival or destruction."
Sun Tzu's The Art of War 1:1:3-4

"Every piece of business strategy acquires its true significance only against the background of that process [of creative destruction] and within the situation created by it. It must be seen in its role in the perennial gale of creative destruction; it cannot be understood irrespective of it or, in fact, on the hypothesis that there is a perennial lull...."
Joseph Schumpeter'

General Principle: Competitive positions are continuously created and destroyed.

Situation: The problem is that it is difficult to see the continual process of creation and destruction that surrounds us. One of our training exercises is a demonstration of change blindness where we show the version of the same picture where a major feature has been eliminated in one of them. If we flash the picture with a second of white space in between, most people simply cannot see the difference. Similarly, we cannot see the changes taking place around us all the time. We expect conditions to be stable and predictable so we see them that way. Our perception of the world changes much slower than reality. Our mental models of the world are powerful tools when they are in sync with reality, but as they gradually fall out of step with the changes around us, they work less and less well. Positions are created and destroyed by the world's powerful process of change despite the limitations of our perceptions and the rigidity of our mental models.

Opportunity:

Just as there can be no opportunity without change, there can be no opportunity without destruction. Creation and destruction are complementary opposites: one requires the other (3.2.3 Complementary Opposites). For a new era to be born, an old era must die. Every act of creation is also an act of destruction. Creation and destruction are closely tied to the objective and subjective nature of positions (1.2 Subobjective Positions). The stubbornness of our opinions can maintain the reality of institutions long after the reality of their value has faded away (1.1.1 Position Dynamics).

One of the my favorite Sun Tzu strategists, Colonel John Boyd, wrote a paper on the role of creation and destruction in strategy. He saw the issue as primarily one of our subjective understanding of situations.

As we have said before, a position consists of two components: a physical reality and a subjective understanding of it. Boyd saw that, as we necessarily learned more, our existing understanding of a position was necessarily destroyed as we come to a higher level of awareness. As he wrote:

> *To comprehend and cope with our environment we develop mental patterns or concepts of meaning. The*

*purpose of this paper is to sketch out how we destroy
and create these patterns to permit us to both shape and
be shaped by a changing environment. In this sense,
the discussion also literally shows why we cannot avoid
this kind of activity if we intend to survive on our own
terms. The activity is dialectic in nature generating both
disorder and order that emerges as a changing and
expanding universe of mental concepts matched to a
changing and expanding universe of observed reality.*

So this creation and destruction of positions is, at its root, a
necessary by-product of our learning. If we don't learn, our competitor's certainly will. We can either destroy our own positions by
advancing them or we can wait for our competitors to destroy our
position by catching up to us and surpassing us.

Key Methods:

The cycles by which positions are advanced not only creates new
positions, but destroys old ones. Strategy exists to save us from the
trap of thinking that the natural order of things is stable. Any stability in any competitive arena is just temporary, a temporary respite
from the battle, nothing more. If the world was stable, we wouldn't
need strategy.

1. Positions are continuously created and destroyed. We must
move forward. We have no choice. We are all crossing the river,
jumping from ice floe to ice floe, before they are swept away or melt
from beneath us. As Sachel Paige said, "Don't look back. Something may be gaining on you." (1.1.1 Position Dynamics)

*2. Creation and destruction begins and ends with our mental
paradigms.* Reality is continuously dynamic, but the human mind
adjusts only in fits and starts. Our mental models, that paradigms
explaining how the world works, are destroyed only after evidence
mounts over time against them and new, better models are found.
Those new, better paradigms are the basis for a new round of cre-
ations and destruction (2.2.2 Mental Models).

3. Periods of stability are temporary illusions. Because perception changes more slowly than reality, positions can seem set in

stone. Every competitive arena--every country, industry, business, and person--may experience a period of quiet where the positions within it are stable. It is only a matter of time until this illusion of stability is destroyed (1.2 Subobjective Positions).

4. Positions that cannot adopt the new paradigm are destroyed. The computer revolution of the late twentieth century changed so many rules about how the world works, that it was only a matter of time until those changes caught up with us, wiping out a generation of organizations that were based on old rules that no long applied (2.1.3 Strategic Deception).

5. Positions grow under the emerging paradigm. As thinking shifts to the new paradigm, the value of these positions are better understood and more broadly appreciated (3.2 Opportunity Creation).

Illustration:

This is a particularly important lesson in today's climate of economic turmoil. We are witnessing the passing of an era where governments and large financial corporations thought that they were the master's of the universe because they were counting on the future being like the past, the trend line of, in this case, real estate prices continuing upward predictably forever. Unfortunately that never happens. Once everyone thinks prices are going up forever, that idea gets factored into the price, which means that the price is too high and the objective reality of what people can afford to pay will re-balance the scale.

1. Positions are continuously created and destroyed. The world's largest financial institutions and car manufacturers, the ones that are "too large to fail," are still in the process of being destroyed while smaller organizations who are more in touch with true risk and value are growing up to replace them.

2. Creation and destruction begins and ends with our mental paradigms. The endangered institutions were based on increasingly flawed economic models based upon the premise that the government could control certain factors, such as how affordable houses were or the standards for corporate accountability, that it could not be controlled.

3. Periods of stability are temporary illusions. Financial institutions and risky loans continued to grow for over a decade, but since the foundation of this growth was based upon broadly held misconceptions rather than financial reality, it was doomed. Organizations that aren't really advancing their positions, go the way of the Soviet Union, the buggy whip industry, Digital Equipment Corporation, and every worker who has lost his or her job by staying with a doomed industry.

4. Positions that cannot adopt the new paradigm are destroyed. The computer revolution of the late twentieth century changed so many rules about how the world works, that it was only a matter of time until those changes caught up with us, wiping out a generation of organizations that were based on old rules that no long applied.

5. Positions grow under the emerging paradigm. New financial organizations will base investments upon the real performance of the underlying assets, not upon the trust in organizations, including the government, who try to package and sell investments disconnected from financial reality.

1.8.2 The Adaptive Loop

Sun Tzu's nine key methods on the continual reiteration of position analysis.

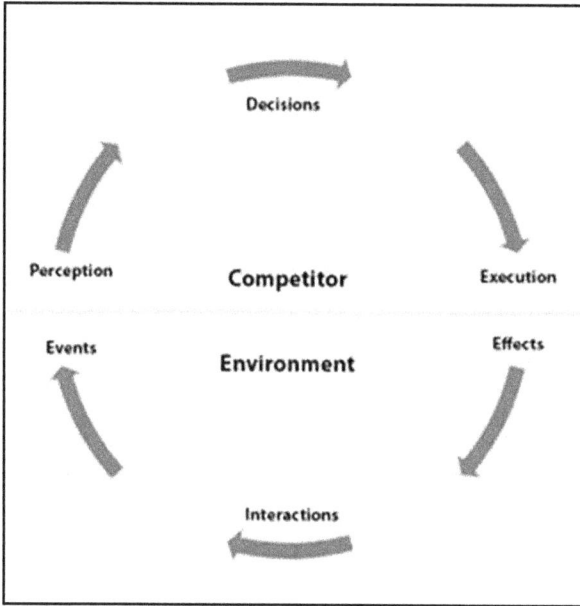

"Military leaders must be experts in knowing how to
adapt to find an advantage. This will teach you the use of
war."

Sun Tzu's The Art of War 8:1:14-15

"We can learn from experience if we are ready to adapt
that experience to changed conditions."

J. C. Masterman

General Principle: Our picture of competitive situations is continually assembled over time.

Situation:

Our challenge is that we are never done adapting to changing conditions. We are flooded with information about change on a daily basis. On what information can we base our reactions? Without a system for filtering, organizing, and prioritizing that information, we end up with a confused, haphazard view of our strategic situation. We may see some aspects that are important but miss others that are much more important. This challenge is made more difficult by the continual distraction of events. To which events do we adapt? Events demand our attention because they are happening now. What is close to us seems bigger than what is far away so whatever is happening now seems more important than what happened yesterday or the day before. But, from this same logic, what seems so important now will seem less so tomorrow. The challenge is knowing which events are important and which are merely urgent.

Opportunity:

The system of elemental analysis gives us all the pieces we need to assemble a meaningful picture of our situation (1.3 Elemental Analysis). However, all strategic positions are paths, constantly moving (1.1 Strategic Paths, 1.1.1 Position Dynamics). Every time we formally analyze strategic positions, we are just getting a snapshot of the situation. That snapshot only shows where positions are now, not how they are changing. We can only see our situations and its opportunities when we assemble this series of snapshots. In doing so, we create a moving picture of the dynamics of the situations. We begin to see not only where positions are, but where they seem to be heading. This dynamic picture is the basis of our situation awareness.

Good situation awareness leads automatically to better decisions. While the other principles of Sun Tzu's strategy are important, even critical in certain situations, they are all based upon having a well-developed sense of situation awareness. We are continually making decisions based on our current level of knowledge, our current understanding of positions.

While we may need to do a formal analysis of strategic positions at certain times for specific reasons, real position awareness has to be a continual process, an integral part of gathering information, making decisions, taking actions, and harvesting the benefits of those actions.

Key Methods:

Living in an adaptive loop is a state of mind that sees the world according to the following key methods.

1. We are continually adapting our picture of our strategic situation and the positions within it. As new information comes in, we update our mental model of the situation, fleshing out our picture of the different missions, climates, grounds, leaders, and methods that affect us. As we move though the cycle of activities needed to advance our position, we continuously adjust our situation awareness. This is not analysis as a separate activity that starts and stops at a certain point in a linear process. It is literally our awareness, the framework within which we are constantly thinking (2.5 The Big Picture).

2. We recognize that the picture is hidden in its pieces. We should be driven by a constant itch that we are missing something important. Our information is always flawed. Our mental models never completely capture objective reality (1.2 Subobjective Positions).

3. We use the five elements as keys to unlock the key aspects of the situation. While we don't know what the strategic picture really looks like, we do know how the five elements fit together within it. By putting together these elements, we start completing blocks of the picture (1.3 Elemental Analysis).

4. We must increase our sense of size and proportion. As we collect more information from a wider variety of sources, we develop perspective, fitting the blocks of elements together, comparing positions. We see that picture from different perspectives. A well-rounded picture of the relationships among positions (2.0 Developing Perspective).

5. We must improve our ability to see where the pieces fit. As we build up our strategic picture, it gets easier and easier to add new pieces of information to it. As the picture takes form, we can see where new pieces of information fit more easily. We see where they reinforce the existing picture (2.6 Information Leverage).

6. We must develop our strategic awareness as an increasingly automatic, background sense. Through practice, we train our minds to sort incoming information. At first, we must do this consciously, working at it. Through practice, however, the process gradually becomes automatic, where we don't have to think about it because it is a habit (6.1.1 Instant Reflexes).

7. Though we can't always see it, we must sense that positions are always changing. Over time, adjusting the picture becomes habit. Things are changing whether we are looking at them or not. They are changing even when we are looking at them and can't see them changing (1.1.1 Position Dynamics).

8. We must sharpen our recognition of when pieces don't fit. As the picture takes shape, information that doesn't fit stands out. Misfit pieces can only be explained one of three ways: either our picture was wrong, the information is flawed, or the picture has changed (2.1.3 Strategic Deception).

9. We must heighten our awareness of the directions of change. As we assemble a series of snapshots of time, we get a moving picture of the dynamics of the situations: not only where positions are, but where they seem to be heading (1.1 Position Paths).

Illustration:

A good analogy for this process is putting together a jigsaw picture puzzle.

1. We are continually adapting our picture of our strategic situation and the positions within it. We cannot solve the puzzle all at once. We must settle on a method of building up our knowledge in small increments.

2. We recognize that the picture is hidden in its pieces. Picture puzzles make this easy by putting the picture on the cover. Competitive strategy requires assembling the pieces without a picture. The picture is both in the pieces and hidden by them.

3. We use the five elements as keys to unlock the key aspects of the situation. We use edges and colors as clues to assembling a picture puzzle. We start by putting pieces together in blocks of similar edges and colors.

4. We must increase our sense of size and proportion. As we get the edges of the picture puzzle completed, we can start seeing where the other blocks of pieces fit.

5. We must improve our ability to see where the pieces fit. As we build up our picture puzzle, it gets easier and easier to add new pieces because we see where the holes are. We start to recognize common shapes of pieces more readily and it takes less time to find the pieces we need.

6. *We must develop our strategic awareness as an increasingly automatic, background sense.* By practicing putting together puzzles, we sharpen all our recognition abilities. As the picture in the puzzle takes form, the pieces we need start to stand out from the pile. We find ourselves just picking up pieces and putting them right where they belong.

7. Though we can't always see it, we must sense that positions are always changing. This doesn't apply to today's jigsaw picture puzzles, but it suggests a whole new type of toy. Moving picture puzzles on the computer, where the picture is a repeating movie loop instead of a static picture.

8. We must sharpen our recognition of when pieces don't fit. We realize when we get off track by putting together two pieces that don't belong together. When the remaining pieces don't fit into the holes we have, we start looking for what we did wrong. If pieces from another puzzle are in the box, we wouldn't notice it at first, but as our picture takes form, those "wrong" pieces stand out more and more clearly.

9. We must heighten our awareness of the directions of things.
If we had, moving picture puzzles, we would only be able to see
how the movie "ended" after the picture gets put together.

1.8.3 Cycle Time

Sun Tzu's seven key methods regarding the importance of speed in feedback and reaction.

"Mastering speed is the essence of war."
Sun Tzu's The Art of War 11:2:16

"There are no speed limits on the road to excellence."
Anonymous

General Principle: Faster cycle times are the essential element of competition.

Situation:

In the unpredictable environment of competition, situations are unpredictable and turn around quickly. Actions often fail. Rewards are always uncertain. Though certain courses of action are more probable to succeed over time, any given instance can fail, sometimes spectacularly. The problem is that we simply do not have enough information or control in a competitive environment to direct events.

Opportunity:

When we think of all actions as a feedback loop rather than steps in a process, every action succeeds--at least in the sense of giving us more information. Even if the information is "that won't work," we learn from each experience. In using Sun Tzu's Playbook, every action is an experiment, an exploration. If we think of the goal in terms of gathering information, there *are* some things that will always work better, especially when comparing our situation to those of others.

Key Methods:

1. In every aspect of competitive strategy, nothing is more important than speed. This is especially important in the feedback loop. The faster we go through the loop of gathering information, making decisions, taking actions, and establishing positions, the more successful we will be. At each stage of this cycle, the use of speed makes success more likely and puts those who might oppose us at a disadvantage (5.3 Reaction Time).

2. The speed of the entire cycle is called cycle time. Cycle time measures how long it takes us to recognize and respond to the situations with which we are faced. In the adaptive world of strategy, faster cycle times *always* beat slower cycle times (1.8.2 The Adaptive Loop).

3. Speed in gathering information is critical. Since the environment is constantly changing, the older our information, the more out of date it must be. The faster that we acquire information, the more information we can get in the limited amount of time we have to make decisions. We must discover opportunities quickly because all opportunities only last for a limited period of time (3.1.6 Time Limitations).

4. Speed in making decisions is critical. Choosing the exact right form of action isn't nearly as important as deciding quickly so we can test our judgment against reality. Quick decisions require a good starting picture of the situation from which to judge changes. Leaders who cannot quickly recognize high-probability opportunities, react quickly, and choose actions that can be quickly executed are at a serious disadvantage (2.5 The Big Picture, 5.3 Reaction Time,).

5. *Speed in moving is critical*. The faster we move, the harder it is for opponents to respond and adjust to our movements. One of the most important aspects of strategy is situation response, where we recognize and respond the situations instantly (6.1.1 Instant Reflexes, 5.4 Minimizing Action).

6. *Speed in claiming positions is critical*. We cannot get rewarded until we clearly establish our position. The more time that elapses between our accomplishments and our claims of a reward, the less likely we are to get rewarded at all (8.1 Successful Positions).

7. *The faster our cycle time, the more quickly we can correct our course*. Since strategy is based on probabilities, we are going to make wrong decisions along with the correct ones. The faster our cycle time, the less time we waste in incorrect actions and the more quickly we are rewarded for correct actions (1.8.4 Probabilistic Process).

Illustration:

Let us look at how these ideas work when applied to investment.

1. ***In every aspect of competitive strategy, nothing is more important than speed.*** If we are going to be successful in investing, as opposed to lucky, we must respond to the up and down movement of the market. We must buy and sell before others do. If we are behind the market, we will lose money consistently, buying high and selling low.

2. ***The speed of the entire cycle is called cycle time.*** The cycle time of an investment is the time between buying and selling. A fast cycle time depends on the horizons we are working in. A day trader works on a faster cycle than weekly or monthly traders, but both must work ahead of their particular cycle.

3. *Speed in gathering information is critical.* It takes any news affecting an investment time to spread to everyone interested. Investors who get the news first, good or bad, always have an advantage.

4. *Speed in making decisions is critical.* To make good decisions about the news that we get about a particular investment, we have to start with some understanding of what it means to that investment. Without an existing picture of its situation, gathering the information to understand the impact of the news takes too much time.

5. *Speed in moving is critical.* It used to be that private traders were at a real disadvantage as far as executing trades. At one time, it took hours and even days to make an investment.

6. *Speed in claiming positions is critical.* The investment doesn't pay when the investment is made, it pays when the position is claimed or closed out. Taking a ten percent profit in a day is better than waiting a month for a twenty percent gain that may vanish.

7. *The faster our cycle time, the more quickly we can correct our course.* Not all of our trades are going to work. We must get out of our losing positions as quickly as we can. We must limit our losses if we are to profit from our gains.

1.8.4 Probabilistic Process

Sun Tzu's seven key methods regarding the role of chance in strategic processes and systems.

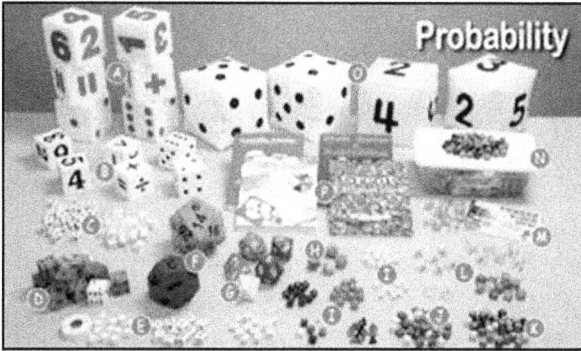

*"Many advantages add up to victory.
Few advantages add up to defeat."*
Sun Tzu's The Art of War 1:5:4-5

*"It is a profitable Wisdom to know when we have
done enough: Much time and Pains are spared, in not
flattering our selves against Probabilities."*
William Penn

General Principle: The adaptive loop leverages probabilities to make success more certain over time.

Situation:

If we expect the adaptive loop to advance our position in a predictable way, we will be disappointed. **Deterministic processes** solve problems working through a predictable linear process. Each step makes a change that gets us closer to our goals, like the steps in the manufacturing process. Every appropriate step has the predicted effect but *only* in a **controlled environment**. This linear thinking doesn't work in competitive environments where outcomes arise from the complex interactions of independent actors with different goals. Since every competitive situation is unique, their outcomes are also unique. Even if we could know all the conditions affecting a situation, outcomes would still be uncertain because the actors involved can create new responses that have never been tried before and whose affects are unknowable.

Opportunity:

Sun Tzu's process is a stochastic process based on probability not a deterministic process. Its probabilities are not fixed. In a competitive environment, we are always prepared for failure because of these uncertainties. We use methods that increase our chances of success over the alternatives but we avoid expensive failure. If we repeat high-probability actions recursively in the adaptive loop the probability of our success increases as long as we can continue to get new tries (1.8 The Adaptive Loop). Though we cannot know *exact* probabilities in the chaotic, competitive environment, we can know when one set of decisions have a higher probability of success than the alternative. The best strategic actions in a competitive environment have the desired effect more frequently than any alternative action.

Key Methods:

We identify higher-probabilities options over lower-probabilities options by using the following set of criteria. We increase our probability of success by choosing situations and options:

1. We increase our probability of success by knowing proven competitive methods. Sun Tzu's entire system defines a set of competitive moves that have been proven to work in different situations. It encompasses a large variety of situations, but it does not cover everything. The system simplifies competitive situations so that we can make quick, more correct decisions, taking into account all the major aspects of mission, climate, ground, command, and methods. Like all simplifications, this system can miss critical details, but knowing what works generally in a large variety of situations is the only way to increase our probability of success (1.3 Elemental Analysis).

2. We increase our chance of success over time by minimizing the impact of our failures. Since our information is always imperfect and our methods are generic, we will have failures. The key is to minimize the costs of those failures so that we get as many attempts as possible. We combine high probability methods with low-cost failures to increase the probability that we will find a way to succeed over time (5.0 Minimizing Mistakes).

3. We can know that high probability opportunities must minimize conflict because conflict is always costly. Logically, our success is more likely if no opponents are trying to stop us. Humans are endlessly creative. Creativity is the wild card in competitive probability. We want people to use their creativity in supporting us because we can never tell what our opponents will try (3.1.3 Conflict Cost)

4. We increase our chance of success by selecting relatively more solid information. Solid information means less complicated and more certain information. Information in competitive environments is always limited. Sun Tzu's entire system focuses our attention on just five key elements and other limited descriptions of situations. It is designed to solidify our information. We must avoid situations and choices with a larger number of unknowns or too much complexity (2.1.1 Information Limits).

5. We increase our ability to predict outcomes when we deal with relatively fewer people. The more people whose actions and reactions can affect the situation and its outcome, the less probability there will be that we get the results that we desire. In Sun Tzu's system, we focus more on those who judge our position than all our potential competitors because that group of potential supporters is usually much smaller (4.5.1 Area).

6. We increase our ability to predict outcomes when people have relatively few choices. The more number of choices the people involved have, the less probable every situation becomes. The minimum number of choices is always two: reaction or non-action. Much of Sun Tzu's system is designed to focus on a single, correct response to a single, dominant aspect of the situation (2.3.3 Range of Reactions).

7. We increase our ability to predict outcomes when we know people's natural tendencies. While every person is different, human psychology has certain tendencies. Our knowledge of tendencies comes primarily from the history of competitive experience and rules that have been developed from that experience (2.3.2 Reaction Unpredictability).

Illustration:

Let us look at these principles from the simple perspective of money management.

1. We increase our probability of our success by knowing proven competitive methods. Mathematically, probabilities mount over time like interest. Small differences at each iteration mount dramatically over time. For example, the difference between 8% and 11% annual interest on $1,000 over twenty years is the difference between $64,000 and a $1,000,000. Similarly, a method that has a 1.1% chance of success will be dramatically more successful than one with a .8% chance of success over twenty years.

2. We increase our chance of success over time by minimizing the impact of our failures. We build for diversified portfolios because we do not want to put all our eggs in one basket. We should avoid investing any sum that we cannot lose in speculative ventures whose value could go to zero.

3. We can know that high probability opportunities must minimize conflict because conflict is always costly. We avoid investing in firms that are in competitive battles where there will be clear winners and losers.

4. We increase our chance of success by selecting relatively more solid information. Personally, I stick to investing in ETFs rather than stocks in individuals firms because information is much better about what is happening within an industry as opposed to what is happening inside a business.

5. *We increase our ability to predict outcomes when we deal with relatively fewer people.* Again, by investing in ETFs, we reduce the impact of individuals on our investments. What happens to the price of Apple if Steve Jobs dies tomorrow? While the probabilities of Job's death are small over the short run, they are certain over the long run.

6. *We increase our ability to predict outcomes when people have relatively few choices.* Again, the dozens of different market sectors represented by ETFs represent a much smaller population than the tens of thousands of different stocks and bonds. In choosing all those stocks, people are choosing among relatively few market segments.

7. *We increase our ability to predict outcomes when we know people's natural tendencies.* There is a natural balance of forces in markets. When a certain investment goes up too quickly, people start developing a desire to sell and collect their profits. Even good investments will temporarily turn around when they are overbought. If we study the natural swings between various sectors, we see the cycle of these swings.

1.9.0 Competition and Production

Sun Tzu's seven key methods regarding the two opposing skill sets of competition and production.

"Supporting the military makes the nation powerful.
Not supporting the military makes the nation weak."
                    Sun Tzu's The Art of War 3:4:**3-4**

"There will be hunters and hunted, winners and losers.
What counts in global competition is the right strategy
and success."
                              Heinrich von Pierer

General Principle: Competition is the complementary opposite of production.

Situation:

In the last several decades, the term "strategy" has been increasingly associated with planning and management control. The problem is that this confuses internal production with external competition. Production and competition are **complementary opposite** skill sets. Sun Tzu described the productive half of this dynamic as the "nation" and the competitive half as the "army." He warns that there is a tremendous danger in not clearly separating these two very different and yet complementary methodologies. In **recent decades** our focus of production has greatly overshadowed our understanding of competition. And, as the principles of complementary opposites requires, this imbalance creates a shift in the environment. Two centuries of advances in production have led to both the atrophy of competitive skills and the worldwide spread of production knowledge. At this point, we have diminishing returns from improving production, so the key advantages are shifting back to the competition side of the equation.

Opportunity:

Production and competition work together. Our opportunity is understanding when to use which set of skills. Our productive skills make the most of the resources that we control, but our competitive skills extend our span of control into new areas with additional resources. Production efficiencies can create a competitive advantage, but when production skills are equal, our advantage is in competitive positioning in the shared environment (1.2.1 Competitive Landscapes). Efficient production requires designing and planning systems. Effective competition requires making creative decisions about how to position ourselves in complex, fast-changing environments (7.3.3 Creative Innovation). Since competitive skills are relatively rare, studying Sun Tzu's methods has become increasingly valuable.

Key Methods:

We use the following seven key methods to use the differences between competition and production.

1. Choosing the right methods requires knowing boundaries between competition and production. The methods of competition--adaptive thinking, expert decision-making, and big-picture problem solving--are very different from the methods of production—linear thinking, process planning, reductionist problems solving. Each set of methods only works well within the appropriate arena (1.5.2. Group Methods).

2. Competition adapts to external environments while production controls internal environments. Competitive interactions are independent decisions while productive interactions are set procedures. This makes the external environment chaotic and unpredictable while the internal environment is organized and more predictable (1.4 The External Environment).

3. Competition generally improves a human position while production shapes resources in a well-specified way. When we deal with those outside of our organization, we must think in terms of relative positioning. When we develop a position, we must think in terms of reshaping what we can control (1.1 Position Paths).

4. Competitive methods explore and experiment while productive methods organize and systematize. Exploration is necessary because competitive resources are unproven. In contrast, productive resources are known and available. We need to explore a new area to discover its value. We need to experiment with a situation to its true nature (1.2.2 Exploiting Exploration).

5. Competitive responses are event driven while productive steps are predetermined. In chaotic environments where actors are free to make their own decisions, we must adapt to events that arise unexpectedly at any time. In controlled environments, most events result from plans, which result from earlier agreements (5.1.1 Event Pressure).

6. *Competition integrates details into a big picture while production reduces large process into detailed steps*. The reductionist methods of production work so well because the environment is controlled and stable. This gives us the luxury of time for even more detailed analysis of how systems work. In competitive environments, we have neither the detailed information needed for reductionist methods nor the time to collect it. Situations simply change too quickly. Instead, we need to quickly develop a big, picture situation awareness that allows us to determine the dominant characteristic of a situation (2.5 The Big Picture).

7. *Competition requires unique, custom solutions while production creates duplicate, standardized results*. In competition, we must develop unique, custom solutions to a unique set of conditions. Since productive methods are based on duplication, they are easily copied, spreading through the environment. Since competitive methods are essentially creative, they create positions that cannot be exactly duplicated (7.3.3 Creative Innovation).

Illustration:

Let us illustrate these seven key methods with illustrations from a variety of competitive environments.

1. *Choosing the right methods requires knowing boundaries between competition and production*. A manager uses strategic skills finding and hiring the best people but he or she uses production skills in assigning them their duties and responsibilities.

2. *Competition adapts to external environments while production controls internal environments*. In our careers, we use strategic skills to search for a better job or get promoted, but we use production skills to get work from our in-box to our out-box.

3. *Competition generally improves a human position while production shapes resources in a well-specified way*. A salesperson uses strategic skills in working with customers but production skills covering his territory and reporting to his superiors.

4. *Competitive methods explore and experiment while productive methods organize and systematize*. In our personal life, we use strategic skills to find and develop our romantic relationships, but we use production skills to maintain a household.

5. Competitive responses are event driven while productive steps are predetermined. Usually only members of a highly bureaucrat organization can get pay raises and promotions in a predictable, pre-planned way. For those of us who want to move up within an organization more quickly than others, we must take advantage of openings that arise unexpectedly within the organization.

6. Competition integrates details into a big picture while production reduces large process into detailed steps. A salesperson can increase their control over a sales process by getting customer agreement to a specific set of detailed steps in the purchasing process. However, to make that process work, the salesperson must first choose the best possible prospect and overall sales strategy which requires a big picture perspective.

7. Competition requires unique, custom solutions while production creates duplicate, standardized results. Apple's competitive methods have created a unique position for them in the high-tech market, but their production methods create reliable, dependable products. A lot of people create unique, dependable products, but it is Apple's unique market position that makes their products more desirable.

1.9.1 Production Comparisons

Sun Tzu's six key methods describing how production naturally creates competition.

"Position yourself where you cannot lose. Never waste an opportunity to defeat your enemy."
Sun Tzu's The Art of War 4:3:22-23

"Our life is not really a mutual helpfulness; but rather, it's fair competition cloaked under due laws of war; it's a mutual hostility."

Thomas Carlyle

General Principle: Success in production is only determined through competitive comparison.

Situation:

Why is competition necessary for production? Can't we just be productive without being competitive? Such thinking represents a serious confusion about what competition and production are and how they depend upon each other. This problem starts with the failure to understand that competition is simply a matter of comparison. One of the most important aspects of life is that we compare our productive capacity. The comparison of production necessarily results in competition. The dynamics of comparing production evolves naturally into different levels of comparison. The problem is that most of us fail to understand the feedback loop of production and competition that defines our dynamic world of actions and reactions.

Opportunity:

Competitive arenas are necessarily defined as much by our productive skills as they are by our competitive skills. In the study of Sun Tzu, we focus on the skills of competition because they are much less familiar to us than the methods of production, but our opportunity for winning in competition arises from the unity of both (3.2.3 Complementary Opposites). In modern society, many of our competitive skills have atrophied because so much of competition is based on solely comparing our ability to produce. However, this comparison of productivity must naturally follow the underlying principles of competitive strategy. Our power arises from seeing how we leverage the balance between competition and production. To do this, we must understand all the different levels of competition inherent in the nature of production.

Key Methods:

There are six key methods that describe the competitive comparison of productive capability.

1. All competition is comparison, which includes the comparison of productive capacity. More production comes simply from improving systems, but rewards are won based upon the comparison of the relative value of that production. The five key elements of a strategic position naturally arise from this process of comparing productivity (1.3.1 Competitive Comparison).

2. Competition starts as a comparison of the natural resources of a position. This might be considered the natural state of a position. It compares our basic ability to choose the ground with the best natural resources for our natural capacities. In Sun Tzu's system, ground is the source of all raw materials. The relative quality of our position arises from the fit between our chosen ground and our natural capacities (1.4.2 Ground Features).

3. Competition extends to a comparison of what we produce from our natural resources. What we are able to produce from our resources depends upon our knowledge. We use that knowledge to transform the raw materials of our position into rarer and more valuable products. This is the beginning of that more advanced form of productivity that arises from what Sun Tzu calls "methods" (1.5.2. Group Methods).

4. Competition lengthens as the comparison of reputations for productivity. Our productivity creates not only products but, over time, our reputation. People judge our decision-making abilities based on what they see us produce. These judgments are generalized to include future expectations about the quality of our future decisions. What people are really comparing at this stage is our judgment itself. When positive, these comparisons lead to increased respect and authority in the community (1.5.1 Command Leadership).

5. Competition deepens as the comparison of our relative progress over time. Over time, we can become more productive through both learning and advancing our position. Changing conditions offer us the opportunity to learn and the opportunity to advance. If we see and take advantage of those opportunities, we win access to new resources. This will increase our productivity even more. Our increasing productivity is seen as progress (1.4.1 Climate Shift).

6. Competition evolves into cooperation from the comparison of direction. Once people can see our progress, they can judge our direction. Our direction reveals our goals and values in terms of productivity. If people share our goals and values, they will work with us. Working with others, we can divide our various tasks to further increase our productivity. Shared missions build organizations and relationships (1.6 Mission Values).

Illustration:

Let us look at some examples of competitive arenas based on these principles. Let us illustrate these different types of competition by looking at the increasingly complex aspects of human existence.

1. All competition is comparison, which includes the comparison of productive capacity. Every animate and inanimate object is a point of comparison.

2. Competition starts as a comparison of the natural resources of a position. Even animals are compared on the basis of "the ground" that they choose. Animals that choose better ground, eat better and have more offspring. Their choice of mates is also considered a form of ground, since that choice yields their natural capacities.

3. Competition extends to a comparison of what we produce from our natural resources. Unlike animals, humans consistently use methods to transform their resources into new, more useful products. Primitive humans created tools from the resources in their environment. Males and females in couples represented the first natural division of labor between two skilled specialists.

4. Competition lengthens as the comparison of reputations for productivity. The importance of reputations increased with the emergence of human societies. The larger the social group, the more important reputation became. Reciprocal altruism became intimately connected with reputation. Others shared with you because you shared with them.

5. *Competition deepens as the comparison of our relative progress over time*. This progress led to the competition among different civilizations. As some groups made faster progress than others, they naturally extended their territory into areas previously controlled by less productive groups. Farmers replaced hunters and gathers because their productivity increased faster.

6. *Competition evolves into cooperation from the comparison of direction*. As they found shared goals, groups of families became clans. Groups of clans became cities. Groups of cities became states. States were united based upon shared history, shared beliefs, and shared values.

1.9.2 Span of Control

Sun Tzu's eight key methods regarding the boundaries of competition leadership and production management.

"You must control your field position. It will always strengthen your army."

Sun Tzu's The Art of War 10:3:1-2

"Good fortune is what happens when opportunity meets with planning."

Thomas Alva Edison

General Principle: Planning works narrowly while strategy works broadly.

Situation:

Just as the skills of competition and production are intertwined by the nature of competitive comparisons, they are divided by our span of control. Only within our span of control do we have good information and control of our resources. Both physically and philosophically, the area that we control is relatively tiny when compared to areas we do not control. The most powerful person in the world can utilize only a tiny fraction of the world's resources. We live in a world with almost seven billion people and tens of millions of organizations. Each of these people and all their various organizations have their own spans of control. Each of these overlapping spans represents limits of information and capability.

Opportunity:

Production opportunities lie inside our area of control. Competitive opportunities lie outside our area of control. Our area of control is tiny compared to the vast expanse of areas where we have no control. This means that most opportunities lie outside of our span of control, where we cannot use the method of production to improve our position. A little circle of light represents where our skills at organization and production matter, and a vast ocean of darkness represents where our skills in positioning and competition matter. The good news is that this means that there are almost an infinite number of strategic opportunities. The challenge is discovering them, which is why so many of the principles of strategy involve collecting and filtering information.

Key Methods:

The eight key methods for resolving the challenges describe a repeating cycle of expansion and contraction.

1. We must listen to expand our strategic perspective. The appropriate strategy to deal with the vast amount of strategic area is a cyclic process of expansion and contraction. Starting with expansion, we use our current span of control as the starting point for gathering information to develop perspective on our position in the larger environment (2.0 Developing Perspective).

2. We then must focus our listening on identifying opportunities*. We follow this broad perspective development by narrowing our focus. We must focus our listening to identify the opportunities in our external environment for advancing our position (3.0 Identifying Opportunities).

3. We aim to expand our position into the opening of the best opportunity*. Improving our position within our tiny area of control requires more and more detailed knowledge about what we control. Because of the scope of the external environment, getting more and more *detailed* information about everything is impossible. We need to pick our best opportunity so we can focus on improving our knowledge of that area. This learning increases our chances of gaining control (4.0 Leveraging Probability).

4. We then focus our aim to minimizing our mistakes in exploring opportunities. This process is like breathing, expanding and contracting. We first broaden our knowledge in a specific direction, but then we must select only one action to focus our actions. We then narrow the scope of our activities to make the most of our resources (5.0 Minimizing Mistakes).

5. We move to expand our position by leveraging the conditions that we discover. As we cross the boundary into areas outside of our span of control, we discover new situations and sets of conditions. To move under these conditions, we must respond appropriately to these conditions (6.0 Situation Response).

6. We then focus our moves on innovation to create momentum. While appropriate methods are needed to start a move, innovation is needed to create the momentum necessary to complete it. This focus on innovation requires the courage of commitment to win the control of new position (7.0 Creating Momentum).

7. We claim to expand the rewards from a new position. Getting control of a position doesn't make it a valuable addition to our span of control. It must generate resources which we can control to produce value (8.0 Winning Rewards).

8. We then focus our claim to defend the value of our positions. This is the last step in the process, by which we consolidate our gains. At this point, we have expanded our span of control, but we must invest in activities that protect it (9.0 Using Vulnerability).

Illustration:

Let us illustrate these ideas by comparing the general business approach to expanding a business with the more specific sales problem of winning a single customer order.

1. We must listen to expand our strategic perspective. In business, we listen to discover how others see our market and how it is changing. In sales, we first listen to discover the broad needs of a customer.

2. We then must focus our listening on identifying opportunities. In business, we focus on identifying the best of new market opportunities. In sales, we focus to identify specific needs that our products can easily fulfill.

3. We aim to expand our position into the opening of the best opportunity. In business, we aim to expand picking the best market opportunity. In sales, we aim to expand our number of orders by meeting more of the customer's needs.

4. We then focus our aim to minimizing our mistakes in exploring opportunities. In business, we identify products and services that we can offer to test a small part of that opportunity. In sales, we aim to win the smallest possible commitment from the customer.

5. We move to expand our position by leveraging the conditions that we discover. In business, we expand by offering products and services to meet customers' unmet needs. In sales, we move by making a proposal to the customer that they can readily appreciate.

6. We then focus our moves on innovation to create momentum. In business, we offer something different to win customers away from alternatives. In sales, we use a novel approach to set up the close.

7. *We claim to expand the rewards from a new position.* In business, we use our new market position to create profitable sales. In sales, we ask for the order.

8. *We then focus our claim to defend the value of our positions*. In business, we focus on defending our new market positions and customers from arising vulnerabilities. In sales, we focus by making sure the order is handled well.

Glossary of Key Concepts from Sun Tzu's *The Art of War*

This glossary is keyed to the most common English words used in the translation of *The Art of War*. Those terms only capture the strategic concepts generally. Though translated as English nouns, verbs, adverbs, or adjectives, the Chinese characters on which they are based are totally conceptual, not parts of speech. For example, the character for conflict is translated as the noun "conflict," as the verb "fight," and as the adjective "disputed." Ancient written Chinese was a conceptual language, not a spoken one. More like mathematical terms, these concepts are primarily defined by the strict structure of their relationships with other concepts. The Chinese names shown in parentheses with the characters are primarily based on Pinyin, but we occasionally use Cantonese terms to make each term unique.

Advance (*Jeun* 進): to move into new **ground**; to expand your **position**; to move forward in a campaign; the opposite of **flee**.

Advantage, *benefit* (*Li* 利)**:** an opportunity arising from having a better **position** relative to an **enemy**; an opening left by an **enemy**; a **strength** that matches against an **enemy's weakness**; where fullness meets emptiness; a desirable characteristic of a strategic **position**.

Aim, *vision, foresee* (*Jian* 見)**: focus** on a specific **advantage**, opening, or opportunity; predicting movements of an **enemy**; a skill of a **leader** in observing **climate**.

Analysis, *plan* (*Gai* 計): a comparison of relative **position**; the examination of the five factors that define a strategic **position**; a combination of **knowledge** and **vision**; the ability to see through **deception**.

Army: see **war.**

Attack, *invade* (*Gong* 攻): a movement to new **ground**; advancing a strategic **position**; action against an **enemy** in the sense of moving into his **ground**; opposite of **defend**; does not necessarily mean **conflict**.

Bad, *ruined* (*Pi* 圮): a condition of the **ground** that makes **advance** difficult; destroyed; terrain that is broken and difficult to traverse; one of the nine situations or types of terrain.

Barricaded: see **obstacles.**

Battle (*Zhan* 戰): to challenge; to engage an **enemy;** generically, to meet a challenge; to choose a confrontation with an **enemy** at a specific time and place; to focus all your resources on a task; to establish superiority in a **position**; to challenge an **enemy** to increase **chaos**; that which is **controlled** by **surprise**; one of the four forms of **attack;** the response to a **desperate situation;** character meaning was originally "big meeting," though later took on the meaning "big weapon"; not necessarily conflict.

Bravery, *courage* (<u>Yong</u> 勇): the ability to face difficult choices; the character quality that deals with the changes of **CLIMATE;** courage of conviction; willingness to act on vision; one of the six characteristics of a leader.

Break, *broken*, *divided* (<u>Po</u> 破): to **divide** what is **complete**; the absence of a **uniting philosophy**; the opposite of <u>unity</u>.

Calculate, *count* (<u>Shu</u> 數): mathematical comparison of quantities and qualities; a measurement of **distance** or troop size.

Change, *transform* (<u>Bian</u> 變): transition from one **condition** to another; the ability to adapt to different situations; a natural characteristic of **climate**.

Chaos, *disorder* (<u>Juan</u> 亂): **conditions** that cannot be **foreseen**; the natural state of confusion arising from **battle**; one of six weaknesses of an organization; the opposite of **control**.

Claim, *position*, *form* (<u>Xing</u> 形): to use the **ground**; a shape or specific condition of **ground**; the **ground** that you **control**; to use the benefits of the **ground**; the formations of troops; one of the four key skills in making progress.

Climate, *heaven* (<u>Tian</u> 天): the passage of time; the realm of uncontrollable **change**; divine providence; the weather; trends that **change** over time; generally, the future; what one must **aim** at in the future; one of five key factors in **analysis;** the opposite of **ground**.

Command (<u>Ling</u> 令): to order or the act of ordering subordinates; the decisions of a **leader**; the creation of **methods**.

Competition: see <u>war.</u>

Complete: see <u>unity.</u>

Condition: see ground.

Confined, *surround* (<u>Wei</u> 圍): to encircle; a **situation** or **stage** in which your options are limited; the proper tactic for dealing with an **enemy** that is ten times smaller; to seal off a smaller **enemy**; the characteristic of a **stage** in which a larger **force** can be attacked by a smaller one; one of nine **situations** or **stages**.

Conflict, *fight* (<u>Zheng</u> 争): to contend; to dispute; direct confrontation of arms with an **enemy**; highly desirable **ground** that creates disputes; one of nine types of **ground,** terrain, or stages.

Constricted, *narrow* (<u>Ai</u> 狹): a confined space or niche; one of six field positions; the limited extreme of the dimension distance; the opposite of **spread-out**.

Control, *govern* (<u>Chi</u> 治): to manage situations; to overcome disorder; the opposite of **chaos**.

Dangerous: see **serious**.

Dangers, *adverse* (Ak 阨): a condition that makes it difficult to **advance**; one of three dimensions used to evaluate advantages; the dimension with the extreme field **positions** of **entangling** and **supporting**.

Death, *desperate* (Si 死): to end or the end of life or efforts; an extreme situation in which the only option is **battle**; one of nine **stages** or types of **terrain**; one of five types of **spies**; opposite of **survive**.

Deception, *bluffing, illusion* (Gui 詭): to control perceptions; to control information; to mislead an **enemy**; an attack on an opponent's **aim**; the characteristic of war that confuses perceptions.

Defend (Shou 守): to guard or to hold a **ground**; to remain in a **position**; the opposite of **attack**.

Detour (Yu 迂): the indirect or unsuspected path to a **position**; the more difficult path to **advantage**; the route that is not **direct**.

Direct, *straight* (Jik 直): a straight or obvious path to a goal; opposite of **detour**.

Distance, *distant* (Yuan 遠): the space separating **ground**; to be remote from the current location; to occupy **positions** that are not close to one another; one of six field positions; one of the three dimensions for evaluating opportunities; the emptiness of space.

Divide, *separate* (Fen 分): to break apart a larger force; to separate from a larger group; the opposite of **join** and **focus**.

Double agent, *reverse* (Fan 反): to turn around in direction; to change a situation; to switch a person's allegiance; one of five types of spies.

Easy, *light* (Qing 輕): to require little effort; a **situation** that requires little effort; one of nine **stages** or types of terrain; opposite of **serious**.

Emotion, *feeling* (Xin 心): an unthinking reaction to **aim**, a necessary element to inspire **moves**; a component of esprit de corps; never a sufficient cause for **attack**.

Enemy, *competitor* (Dik 敵): one who makes the same **claim**; one with a similar **goal;** one with whom comparisons of capabilities are made.

Entangling, *hanging* (Gua 懸): a **position** that cannot be returned to; any **condition** that leaves no easy place to go; one of six field positions.

Evade, *avoid* (Bi 避): the tactic used by small competitors when facing large opponents.

Fall apart, *collapse* (Beng 崩): to fail to execute good decisions; to fail to use a **constricted** position; one of six weaknesses of an organization.

Fall down, *sink* (Haam 陷): to fail to make good decisions; to **move** from a **supporting position**; one of six weaknesses of organizations.

Feelings, *affection, love* (_Ching_ 情): the bonds of relationship; the result of a shared **philosophy**; requires management.

Fight, *struggle* (Dou 鬥): to engage in **conflict**; to face difficulties.

Fire (_Huo_ 火): an environmental weapon; a universal analogy for all weapons.

Flee, *retreat, northward* (_Bei_ 北): to abandon a **position**; to surrender **ground**; one of six weaknesses of an **army**; opposite of **advance**.

Focus, *concentrate* (_Zhuan_ 專): to bring resources together at a given time; to **unite** forces for a purpose; an attribute of having a shared **philosophy**; the opposite of *divide*.

Force (_Lei_ 力): power in the simplest sense; a **group** of people bound by **unity** and **focus**; the relative balance of **strength** in opposition to **weakness**.

Foresee: see **aim**.

Fullness: see **strength**.

General: see **leader**.

Goal: see **philosophy**.

Ground, *situation, stage* (_Di_ 地): the earth; a specific place; a specific condition; the place one competes; the prize of competition; one of five key factors in competitive analysis; the opposite of **climate**.

Groups, *troops* (_Dui_ 隊): a number of people united under a shared **philosophy**; human resources of an organization; one of the five targets of fire attacks.

Inside, *internal* (_Nei_ 內): within a **territory** or organization; an insider; one of five types of spies; opposite of _Wai_, outside.

Intersecting, *highway* (_Qu_ 衢): a **situation** or **ground** that allows you to **join**; one of nine types of terrain.

Join (_Hap_ 合): to unite; to make allies; to create a larger **force**; opposite of **divide**.

Knowledge, *listening* (_Zhi_: 知): to have information; the result of listening; the first step in advancing a **position**; the basis of strategy.

Lax, *loosen* (_Shii_ 弛): too easygoing; lacking discipline; one of six weaknesses of an army.

Leader, *general, commander* (_Jiang_ 將): the decision-maker in a competitive unit; one who **listens** and **aims**; one who manages **troops**; superior of officers and men; one of the five key factors in analysis; the conceptual opposite of _fa_, the established methods, which do not require decisions.

Learn, *compare* (_Xiao_ 效): to evaluate the relative qualities of **enemies**.

Listen, *obey* (_Ting_ 聽): to gather **knowledge**; part of **analysis**.

Listening: see **knowledge.**

Local, *countryside* (<u>Xiang</u> 鄉): the nearby **ground**; to have **knowledge** of a specific **ground**; one of five types of **spies**.

Marsh (<u>Ze</u> 澤): **ground** where footing is unstable; one of the four types of **ground**; analogy for uncertain situations.

Method: see **system.**

Mission: see **philosophy.**

Momentum, *influence* (<u>Shi</u> 勢): the **force** created by **surprise** set up by **standards;** used with **timing.**

Mountains, *hill, peak* (<u>Shan</u> 山):uneven **ground**; one of four types of **ground**; an analogy for all unequal **situations.**

Move, *march, act* (<u>Hang</u> 行): action toward a position or goal; used as a near synonym for <u>dong</u>, act.

Nation (<u>Guo</u> 國): the state; the productive part of an organization; the seat of political power; the entity that controls an **army** or competitive part of the organization.

Obstacles, *barricaded* (<u>Xian</u> 險): to have barriers; one of the three characteristics of the **ground**; one of six field positions; as a field position, opposite of **unobstructed.**

Open, *meeting, crossing* (<u>Jiao</u> 來): to share the same **ground** without conflict; to come together; a **situation** that encourages a race; one of nine **terrains** or **stages.**

Opportunity: see <u>advantage.</u>

Outmaneuver (<u>Sou</u> 走): to go astray; to be **forced** into a **weak position**; one of six weaknesses of an army.

Outside, *external* (<u>Wai</u> 外): not within a **territory** or **army**; one who has a different perspective; one who offers an objective view; opposite of **internal.**

Philosophy, *mission, goals* (<u>Tao</u> 道): the shared **goals** that **unite** an **army**; a system of thought; a shared viewpoint; literally "the way"; a way to work together; one of the five key factors in **analysis.**

Plateau (<u>Liu</u> 陸): a type of **ground** without defects; an analogy for any equal, solid, and certain **situation**; the best place for competition; one of the four types of **ground.**

Resources, *provisions* (<u>Liang</u> 糧): necessary supplies, most commonly food; one of the five targets of fire attacks.

Restraint: see **timing.**

Reward, *treasure, money* (*Bao* 賞): profit; wealth; the necessary compensation for competition; a necessary ingredient for **victory**; **victory** must pay.

Scatter, *dissipating* (*San* 散): to disperse; to lose **unity**; the pursuit of separate **goals** as opposed to a central **mission**; a situation that causes a **force** to scatter; one of nine conditions or types of terrain.

Serious, *heavy* (*Chong* 重): any task requiring effort and skill; a **situation** where resources are running low when you are deeply committed to a campaign or heavily invested in a project; a situation where opposition within an organization mounts; one of nine **stages** or types of **terrain.**

Siege (*Gong Cheng* 攻城): to move against entrenched positions; any movement against an **enemy's strength**; literally "strike city"; one of the four forms of attack; the least desirable form of attack.

Situation: see **ground.**

Speed, *hurry* (Sai 馳): to **move** over **ground** quickly; the ability to **advance positions** in a minimum of time; needed to take advantage of a window of opportunity.

Spread-out, *wide* (*Guang* 廣): a surplus of **distance**; one of the six **ground positions**; opposite of **constricted.**

Spy, *conduit, go-between* (*Gaan* 間): a source of information; a channel of communication; literally, an "opening between."

Stage: see **ground.**

Standard, *proper, correct* (*Jang* 正): the expected behavior; the standard approach; proven methods; the opposite of surprise; together with **surprise** creates **momentum.**

Storehouse, *house* (*Ku* 庫): a place where resources are stockpiled; one of the five targets for fire attacks.

Stores, *accumulate, savings* (*Ji* 糧):resources that have been stored; any type of inventory; one of the five targets of fire attacks.

Strength, *fullness, satisfaction* (*Sat* 壹): wealth or abundance or resources; the state of being crowded; the opposite of Xu, empty.

Supply wagons, *transport* (Zi 輜): the movement of **resources** through **distance**; one of the five targets of fire attacks.

Support, *supporting* (*Zhii* 支): to prop up; to enhance; a **ground position** that you cannot leave without losing **strength**; one of six field positions; the opposite extreme of gua, entangling.

Surprise, *unusual, strange* (*Qi* 奇) : the unexpected; the innovative; the opposite of **standard**; together with **standards** creates **momentum**.

Surround: see **confined**.

Survive, *live, birth* (*Shaang* 生): the state of being created, started, or beginning; the state of living or surviving; a temporary condition of fullness; one of five types of spies; the opposite of **death**.

System, *method* (*Fa* 法): a set of procedures; a group of techniques; steps to accomplish a **goal**; one of the five key factors in analysis; the realm of groups who must follow procedures; the opposite of the **leader**.

Territory, *terrain*: see **ground**.

Timing, *restraint* (*Jie* 節): to withhold action until the proper time; to release tension; a companion concept to **momentum**.

Troops: see **group**.

Unity, *whole, oneness* (*Yi* 一): the characteristic of a **group** that shares a **philosophy**; the lowest number; a **group** that acts as a unit; the opposite of **divided**.

Unobstructed, *expert* (*Tong* 通): without obstacles or barriers; **ground** that allows easy movement; open to new ideas; one of six field positions; opposite of **obstructed**.

Victory, *win, winning* (*Sing* 勝): success in an endeavor; getting a reward; serving your mission; an event that produces more than it consumes; to make a profit.

War, *competition, army* (**Bing** 兵): a dynamic situation in which **positions** can be won or lost; a contest in which a **reward** can be won; the conditions under which the principles of strategy work.

Water, *river* (*Shui* 水): a fast-changing **ground**; fluid **conditions**; one of four types of **ground**; an analogy for change.

Weakness, *emptiness, need* (*Xu* 虛): the absence of people or resources; devoid of **force**; the point of **attack** for an **advantage;** a characteristic of **ground** that enables **speed**; poor; the opposite of strength.

Win, *winning*: see **victory**.

Wind, *fashion, custom* (*Feng* 風): the pressure of environmental forces.

The *Art of War Playbook* Series

There are over two-hundred and thirty articles on Sun Tzu's competitive principles in the nine volumes of the *Art of War Playbook*. Each volume covers a specific area of Sun Tzu strategy.

About the Translator and Author

Gary Gagliardi is recognized as America's leading expert on Sun Tzu's *The Art of War*. An award-winning author and business strategist, his many books on Sun Tzu's strategy have been translated around the world. He has appeared on hundreds of talk shows nationwide, providing strategic insight on the breaking news. He has trained decision makers from some of the world's most successful organizations in competitive thinking. His workshops convert Sun Tzu's many principles into a series of practical tools for handling common competitive challenges.

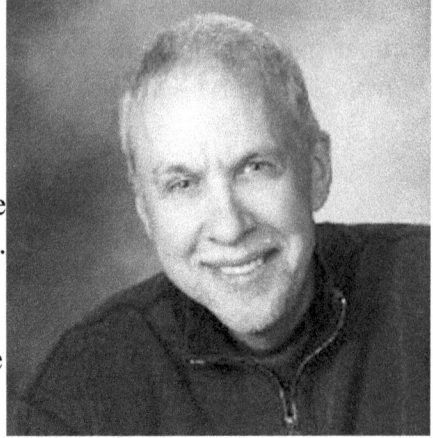

Gary began using Sun Tzu's competitive principles in a successful corporate career and when he started his own software company. In 1990, he wrote his first *Art of War* adaptation for his company's salespeople. By 1992, his company was on *Inc. Magazine's* list of the 500 fastest-growing privately held companies in America. He personally won the U.S. Chamber of Commerce Blue Chip Quality Award and was an Ernst and Young Entrepreneur of the Year finalist. His customers—AT&T, GE, and Motorola, among others—began inviting him to speak at their conferences. After becoming a multimillionaire when he sold his software company in 1997, he continued teaching *The Art of War* around the world.

Gary has authored several breakthrough works on *The Art of War*. Ten of his books on strategy have won book award recognition in nine different non-fiction categories.

Art of War Books by Gary Gagliardi